Feathered Facts: A Trivia Book About Birds

Karen Lee

Copyright © 2023 Karen Lee

All rights reserved.

No portion of this book may be reproduced in any form without written permission from the publisher or author, except as permitted by U.S. copyright law.

ISBN: 9798396628199

To all the bird lovers and enthusiasts who find joy in watching these magnificent creatures and how they fill our world with songs. May this book inspire you to appreciate and protect these fascinating beings and continue exploring the avian world's wonders.

CONTENTS

Introduction viii

Chapter 1: A Bird's Eye View 1
What Is A Bird? 1
What Makes Birds Different from Other Animals? 2
Bird Anatomy 3
Where Are Birds Found? 4
Are There Any Places Birds Aren't Found? 5
Types of Birds 6
What Kind of Birds Are Customarily Eaten? 7
Which Birds Are Endangered? 8
Which Are the Most Common Birds? 10

Chapter 2: Feathered Fascinations:
The Surprising Behaviors of Birds 13
What Are Some Bird Behaviors? 13
What Are Some Migration Patterns? 14
What Are Their Nesting Habits? 16
What Are Their Courtship Rituals? 18
How Do Birds Raise Their Young? 20
What Are Their Feeding Behaviors? 21
How Do Birds Communicate? 23
What Are the Different Kinds of Bird Songs? 24
What Do Bird Songs Mean? 25
Which Birds Are Best at Mimicking Human Speech? 27

Chapter 3: Remarkable and Memorable Birds 28
Who Are the Smallest Birds? 28
Who Are the Largest Birds? 29
Who Are the Heaviest Birds? 31
Who Are the Fastest Birds? 32
Which Birds Have the Most Feathers? 33

What Birds Have the Least Feathers?....................................34
Which Birds Have the Shortest Beaks? 36
Which Birds Have the Longest Beaks? 37
Which Birds Have the Longest Feathers?..............................38
Which Birds Have the Shortest Feet? 40
Which Birds Lay the Smallest Eggs?...................................... 41
Which Birds Lay the Largest Eggs? 43
Which Birds Have the Most Colorful Feathers? 44
Which Birds Have the Longest Names? 46

Chapter 4: Winged Inspiration: Birds in Art, Literature, and Entertainment 48
Bands With Bird Names...48
Bird References in Songs 49
Bird References in Theatre 51
Birds in Poems 53
Birds in Novels 55
Bird References in Art..56
Birds in Movies.. 59
Birds in Television... 61
Birds in Comic Books 63
Birds in Fairy Tales 65
Mythical Birds 67
Birds as Pets 70

Chapter 5: Wandering with Wings: Bird Watching and Appreciation...73
Who Studies Birds? 73
John James Audubon...74
George Bird Grinnell 76
The Audubon Society 77
About Bird Watching...79
Tools for Bird Watching.. 80
Tips for Bird Watching.. 81

Best Locations for Bird Watching 83
More Fun Facts About Bird Watching 84
Are You Interested in Bird Watching? 86
Bird Conservation.. 87
Why Are Birds Important to Our Ecosystem? 88

Thank You **91**
References and Sources **92**
Index **94**

INTRODUCTION

Welcome to "Feathered Facts: A Trivia Book About Birds"! This book is a compilation of fascinating and little-known facts about the avian world. From their unique physical features to their incredible behaviors, birds have captured our attention and imagination for centuries. Whether you are an avid bird watcher, a nature enthusiast, or simply curious about the world around us, this book is for you.

Inside, you will discover intriguing trivia about bird anatomy, behavior, and diversity, as well as their interactions with humans and the environment. Learn about the courtship rituals of various bird species, the amazing ability of some birds to mimic human speech, and birds' critical role in pollination and pest control.

You'll also find helpful tips for successful bird watching and a brief history of this popular pastime. Most importantly, you'll gain a deeper appreciation for the importance of birds in our ecosystem and the need for their conservation.

So, grab a cozy perch, and dive into the fascinating world of birds. You might discover something new and surprising that will leave you in awe of these feathered creatures. Enjoy "Feathered Facts: A Trivia Book About Birds"!

1 A BIRD'S EYE VIEW

What Is A Bird?

Birds are warm-blooded vertebrates with feathers, wings, and beaks. They are found in virtually every part of the world, from deserts and rainforests to mountains and oceans. Some species are migratory and travel thousands of miles each year to breed and feed.

Birds are a diverse group of animals and have adapted to a wide range of environments and diets. Some birds, like eagles and hawks, are carnivorous and feed on other animals, while others, like hummingbirds and sunbirds, feed mainly on nectar. Some birds, like chickens and turkeys, are domesticated and raised for their meat and eggs.

Despite their diversity, all birds have some common characteristics. For example, they all have wings and feathers, which help them to fly, maintain body temperature, and attract mates. They also have a unique respiratory system that allows them to take in oxygen more efficiently during flight. Additionally, birds have a four-chambered heart, which allows them to pump oxygenated blood more effectively to their muscles and organs. Finally, all birds lay eggs as part of their reproductive cycle.

What Makes Birds Different From Other Animals?

Birds have several unique characteristics that set them apart from other animals.

Feathers: Birds are the only animals with feathers. Feathers help birds to fly, regulate their body temperature, and attract mates. They also come in a variety of colors and patterns, which help to identify different species.

Wings: Birds are also the only animals with wings. Their wings are modified forelimbs that allow them to fly, glide, and soar through the air.

Beaks: Birds have beaks instead of teeth, which they use to grasp and manipulate food. The shape and size of a bird's beak are often specialized to its diet and feeding habits.

Lightweight skeletons: Birds have light skeletons filled with air sacs, which reduces their weight and makes it easier for them to fly.

Unique respiratory system: Birds have a unique respiratory system that allows them to take in oxygen more efficiently during flight. They have a set of air sacs that act as bellows, moving air in and out of their lungs and ensuring a constant supply of oxygen.

Strong hearts: Birds have a four-chambered heart, which allows them to pump oxygenated blood more effectively to their muscles and organs. This helps support their high metabolism, which helps their ability to fly long distances.

These unique characteristics allow birds to adapt to a wide range of environments and play essential roles in ecosystems worldwide.

Bird Anatomy

Here are some interesting facts about the anatomy of birds:

Feathers: As mentioned earlier, birds are the only animals with feathers. Feathers are made of keratin, the same material that makes up our hair and nails. Feathers help birds to fly, regulate their body temperature, and attract mates.

Wings: Birds have two wings that are modified forelimbs. The wings are covered in feathers and are used for flight, gliding, and soaring.

Beaks: Birds have beaks instead of teeth, which they use to grasp and manipulate food. The shape and size of a bird's beak are often specialized to its diet and feeding habits.

Hollow Bones: Birds have lightweight, hollow bones that are filled with air sacs, which reduce their weight and make it easier for them to fly.

Four-Chambered Heart: Like mammals, birds have a

four-chambered heart. This allows them to pump oxygenated blood more effectively to their muscles and organs.

Crop: Birds have a specialized pouch in their esophagus called a crop, which they use to store food before digestion. This allows them to eat quickly and then digest their food later when it is safe to do so.

Gizzard: Besides their stomach, birds have a muscular gizzard that helps them grind food. The gizzard contains small rocks or grit that the bird swallows to help break down tough plant material.

These unique anatomical features have allowed birds to adapt to a wide range of environments.

Where Are Birds Found?

Birds are found in virtually every part of the world, including all continents and oceans. Some species are highly adaptable and can be found in many habitats, while others are more specialized and restricted to specific regions.

Forests: Many bird species are found in forests, ranging from the dense tropical rainforests to the coniferous forests of the northern hemisphere.

Grasslands: Open grasslands and savannas are home to a variety of bird species, like ostriches, cranes, and quails.

Wetlands: Wetlands, like marshes, swamps, and estuaries, are important habitats for many bird species, including waterfowl, shorebirds, and wading birds.

Deserts: Some bird species are adapted to arid desert environments, like the roadrunner and the burrowing owl.

Oceans: Seabirds like albatrosses, gulls, and terns spend most of their lives at sea and are found in all oceans of the world.

Urban areas: Many bird species have adapted to living in urban areas, like pigeons, sparrows, and starlings.

Birds are found in many habitats, from the depths of the oceans to the highest mountaintops. Their adaptability has allowed them to thrive in virtually every corner of the world!

Are There Any Places Birds Aren't Found?

Birds are found in almost every part of the world, from the freezing polar regions to the hot deserts and tropical rainforests. However, there are a few places where birds are not commonly found.

Antarctica: While some seabirds and migratory birds visit Antarctica, there are no resident bird populations on the continent itself.

High-altitude peaks: At very high altitudes, like the summit of Mount Everest, the air is too thin for birds to fly. Therefore, birds are not found at these extreme elevations.

Extreme deserts: In extremely arid regions like the Sahara and the Arabian Desert, bird populations may be scarce due to the lack of water and vegetation.

Polar regions during the winter: During the winter months, the Arctic and Antarctic regions are covered in ice and snow, and food is scarce. Many bird species migrate to more hospitable areas during this time, leaving few birds behind.

Even in these places, some birds may survive in harsh conditions, like penguins in Antarctica or high-altitude birds, like the bar-headed goose in the Himalayas.

Types of Birds

There are thousands of different bird species in the world, and they can be categorized into several different groups based on their physical and behavioral characteristics. Here are some of the main types of birds:

Songbirds: Also known as passerines, songbirds are the largest group of birds and make up more than half of all bird species. Songbirds are known for their complex vocalizations and include birds like sparrows, finches, and warblers.

Birds of prey: Also known as raptors, birds of prey are characterized by their sharp talons, hooked beaks, and excellent eyesight. They include eagles, hawks, owls, and falcons.

Waterbirds: Waterbirds include birds that are adapted to living in and around water, like ducks, geese, swans, pelicans, and cormorants.

Gamebirds: Gamebirds are hunted for sport or food, like pheasants, quail, and grouse.

Flightless birds: Flightless birds have lost the ability to fly over time. They include ostriches, emus, kiwis, and penguins.

Seabirds: Seabirds spend most of their lives at sea and include birds like albatrosses, gulls, and terns.

Hummingbirds: Hummingbirds are small, colorful birds known for their ability to hover in mid-air and feed on nectar.

These are just a few examples of the different types of birds, and there are many other categories and subcategories that can be used to group them based on their physical and behavioral characteristics.

What Kind Of Birds Are Customarily Eaten?

Many species of birds are consumed as food around the world.

Chicken: Chicken is one of the most commonly consumed types of poultry worldwide. It is a domesticated bird that is raised for its meat and eggs.

Turkey: Turkey is a large bird that is native to North America. It is often consumed during holidays and special occasions like Thanksgiving and Christmas.

Duck: Duck is a popular food in many parts of the world, particularly in Asian cuisine. The meat is often rich and flavorful and used in various dishes.

Quail: Quail is a small game bird often served as a delicacy. It is known for its tender meat and mild flavor.

Pheasant: Pheasant is another game bird that is often consumed. It has a unique flavor and is commonly used in stews, soups, and other dishes.

Goose: The goose is a large bird often served during holiday feasts, particularly in Europe. It has a rich, fatty meat similar in flavor to duck.

It is important to note that some bird species are protected by law and may not be hunted or consumed. Additionally, the consumption of birds may vary widely by culture and geography, and there may be many other types of birds consumed in different parts of the world.

Which Birds Are Endangered?

Sadly, many bird species are currently endangered or at risk of extinction due to various threats like habitat loss, hunting, and climate change. Here are some of the most endangered birds in the world:

Hawaiian Crow: Also known as the 'Alala, the Hawaiian Crow is a bird native to the Hawaiian Islands. It is critically endangered, with only a few dozen individuals remaining in the wild.

Spoon-billed Sandpiper: This small bird is a wading bird found in parts of Asia. It is considered critically endangered, with fewer than 500 individuals remaining in the wild.

Blue-throated Macaw: This beautiful bird is native to Bolivia and is considered critically endangered due to habitat loss and poaching. It is estimated that there are fewer than 300 individuals left in the wild.

Madagascar Pochard: The Madagascar Pochard is a duck species endemic to Madagascar. It is considered critically endangered, with only a few remaining in the wild.

Philippine Eagle: The Philippine Eagle is a large bird of prey that is found only in the Philippines. It is considered critically endangered, with only around 400 individuals remaining in the wild.

Black Stilt: The Black Stilt is a wading bird native to New Zealand. It is considered critically endangered, with only around 120 individuals remaining in the wild.

Madagascar Fish Eagle: This bird of prey is native to Madagascar and is considered critically endangered due to habitat loss and hunting. It is estimated that fewer than 250 individuals are left in the wild.

Great Indian Bustard: This large bird is native to India and is considered critically endangered due to habitat loss and hunting. It is estimated that there are fewer than 300 individuals left in the wild.

Helmeted Hornbill: This bird is found in parts of Southeast Asia and is considered critically endangered due to habitat loss and poaching. It is estimated that there are fewer than 1,000 individuals left in the wild.

Siberian Crane: The Siberian Crane is a migratory bird found in parts of Asia and Russia. It is considered critically endangered, with only around 3,000 remaining in the wild.

These bird species are just a few examples of the many endangered species around the world. We must take action to protect these species and their habitats to ensure their survival for future generations.

Which Are the Most Common Birds?

The most common birds can vary widely depending on the location and habitat, but here are some of the most widespread and abundant bird species around the world:

House Sparrow: This small bird is native to Eurasia but has been introduced to many other parts of the world. It is one of the most widespread and abundant bird species, with a global population of around 500 million.

European Starling: The European Starling is a bird native to Europe but has been introduced to many other parts of the world, including North America, South Africa, and Australia. It is one of the most common birds in these regions, with a global population of around 200 million.

Rock Pigeon: Also known as the common pigeon or city

pigeon, the Rock Pigeon is found in cities and towns around the world. It is estimated that there are around 400 million individuals worldwide.

Barn Swallow: The Barn Swallow is a migratory bird in many parts of the world, including North America, Europe, and Asia. It is one of the most common and widespread swallow species, with a global population of around 190 million.

American Robin: The American Robin is a bird that is native to North America and is known for its distinctive red breast. It is one of North America's most common and widespread bird species, with a population of around 320 million.

Common Blackbird: The Common Blackbird is found throughout Europe, Asia, and North Africa. It is one of the most common birds in these regions, with a global population of around 250 million.

Mallard: The Mallard is a type of duck found in many parts of the world. It is one of the most common duck species, with a global population of around 30 million.

White-throated Sparrow: This small songbird is found throughout North America and is known for its beautiful singing voice. It is one of the most common bird species in eastern North America.

Red-billed Quelea: The Red-billed Quelea is a small bird found throughout sub-Saharan Africa. It is one of the most abundant bird species in the world, with a global population estimated at over a billion individuals.

Common Kestrel: The Common Kestrel is a small bird of prey found in many parts of the world, including Europe, Asia, and Africa. It is one of the most common and widespread birds of prey in the world.

These are just a few examples of the most common bird species in the world. Many others are abundant in different regions and habitats.

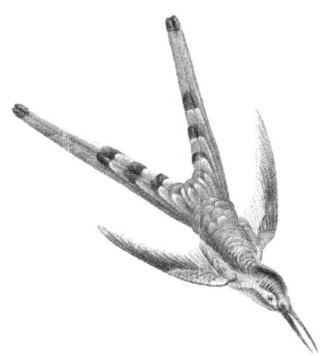

2 FEATHERED FASCINATIONS: THE SURPRISING BEHAVIORS OF BIRDS

What Are Some Bird Behaviors?

Birds exhibit a wide range of behaviors that vary depending on the species and their habitat.

Nest-building: Different species build nests using different materials like twigs, grasses, and mud. Some even dig their nests into the ground.

Mating displays: During mating season, male birds may perform elaborate displays to attract females, like singing, dancing, or displaying their colorful feathers.

Migration: Some birds migrate long distances each year to take advantage of seasonal changes in food and weather conditions.

Foraging: Birds spend a lot of time searching for food. Different species have different foraging behaviors.

Vocalizations: Birds communicate with each other using a variety of vocalizations, including songs, calls, and alarms.

Courtship rituals: Many bird species have complex courtship rituals that involve specific behaviors and displays.

Parental care: Many bird species provide extensive care for their young once their eggs hatch.

Aggression: Birds may exhibit aggressive behaviors when defending their territory or competing for resources.

Tool use: Some bird species, like crows and parrots, are known to use tools to obtain food or build nests.

Bathing: Many species bathe in water to keep their feathers clean and in good condition.

Sunbathing: Some bird species, like vultures and cormorants, sunbathe to help dry their wings and regulate their body temperature.

Sleeping: Birds have different sleeping behaviors depending on the species. Some sleep while perched on branches, while others sleep on the ground.

What Are Some Migration Patterns?

There are several different types of migration patterns for birds:

Short-distance migration: The American Robin, Tree

Swallow, Cedar Waxwing, Black-capped Chickadee, and White-throated Sparrow are short-distance migrators. They migrate relatively short distances — one hundred miles or less. Songbirds, for example, may migrate from northern breeding grounds to southern wintering grounds.

Long-distance migration: The Arctic Tern, Bar-tailed Godwit, Ruby-throated Hummingbird, Osprey, and Sooty Shearwater migrate long distances between their breeding grounds and wintering grounds. This may involve crossing continents or even traveling between hemispheres. Undertaking these remarkable long-distance migrations require incredible endurance and navigational abilities.

Altitudinal migration: Altitudinal migration is a type of bird migration where birds move vertically between different elevations of their habitat, typically in response to seasonal changes in food availability and temperature. White-tailed Ptarmigan, Rufous-tailed Hummingbird, Golden Eagle, and Andean Condor are all altitudinal migrators.

Nomadic migration: Eurasian Wigeon, Snow Bunting, Bohemian Waxwing, Common Crossbill, and Lapland Longspur are nomadic migraters. These birds don't follow fixed migration routes or schedules but rather move in response to localized changes in food availability and weather conditions. Their nomadic nature allows them to take advantage of temporary food sources and suitable habitats, making their movements less predictable compared to birds with regular migration patterns.

Partial migration: Northern Cardinals, Blue Jays, and Red-winged Blackbirds are partial migrators. Partial migration is when only a portion of the population migrates while others remain resident year-round. The decision to migrate or stay can vary within a species depending on factors like food availability, climate, and genetic differences within populations. Partial migration allows a bird to adapt to local conditions while balancing the advantages of migration with the benefits of staying in familiar territories.

Irregular migration: Some bird species do not follow a consistent migration pattern at all and may only migrate in certain years or under certain conditions. Examples are Pine Siskins, Cedar Waxings, American Crows, and Wilson's Warblers. Studying irregular migrators is an exciting challenge for researchers and birdwatchers, as their unpredictable movements make it more difficult to study and track their migratory patterns.

What Are Their Nesting Habits?

Birds exhibit a wide variety of nesting habits, which have evolved over time to meet the specific needs of each species. Understanding these nesting habits can give us insight into the behavior and ecology of different bird species. In this regard, this topic is fascinating and essential for bird enthusiasts and researchers alike.

Ground-nesting: Killdeer, Piping Plovers, Northern Lapwings, and the American Oystercatcher build their nests directly on the ground.

Cavity-nesting: Woodpeckers, Bluebirds, Chickadees, and Tree Swallows nest in natural or artificial cavities in trees or other structures.

Burrow-nesting: Kingfishers, Burrowing Owls, Atlantic Puffins, and European Bee-eaters nest in burrows they dig into the ground or excavate from a bank of earth.

Platform-nesting: Osprey, Bald eagles, Hawks, and Ravens build their nests on a platform of sticks, twigs, and other materials.

Cup-nesting: American Robins, Song Sparrows, and House Finches build cup-shaped nests from materials like grasses, twigs, and feathers.

Hanging-nesting: The Baltimore Oriole, Baya Weaver, and Phoebes build hanging nests suspended from branches or other structures.

Floating or Raft nesting: Coots, Moorhens, and Jacanas build floating nests out of reeds, twigs, and other vegetation. They stay afloat on water.

Cup-and-saucer nesting: Crested Auklets, Rock Sparrows, and Rufous-vented Chachalacas build shallow cup-shaped nests on branches with mud rims. This cup-and-saucer structure gives the nest strength and support.

Adhesive nesting: African Palm Swifts, Grey-rumped Treeswifts, and Rufous Hornero build nests using saliva, mud, and other sticky materials to attach the nest to tree tucks, rocks, and even structures built by humans.

What Are Their Courtship Rituals?

Bird courtship is a complex process involving a variety of behaviors and displays. The specific courtship behaviors can vary widely depending on the species.

Singing: Many bird species use songs as part of their courtship displays. Males may sing complex songs to attract females or to establish and defend their territory.

Dancing: The Greater Sage-Grouse, Red-capped Manakin, and Blue-footed Booby perform elaborate dances as part of their courtship displays. These dances may involve wing displays, hopping, or other movements.

Preening: Birds, like doves, pigeons, and some waterfowls, often preen or groom their feathers as part of their courtship displays. This behavior can be used to show off their plumage and establish dominance.

Gift-giving: The male Bowerbird, Great Crested Grebes, and Gray-headed Albatrosses offer gifts to females as part of their courtship displays.

Nest-building: Male Weaver Birds, Barn Swallows, Eagles, and Woodpeckers build nests as part of their courtship displays. Females may inspect the nest and choose a mate based on the quality of the nest-building.

Displays of color: Peacocks, Birds of Paradise, Eastern Rosellas, and Painted Buntings have brightly colored feathers they use in their courtship displays. Males puff out their feathers or display colorful plumage to attract females.

Chase and capture: Male Red-winged blackbirds, Northern Harriers, American Woodcocks, and Marsh Wrens chase and capture females in their courtship displays. This behavior is intended to impress females and establish a hierarchy among competing males.

Mimicry: The Superb Lyrebird, Satin Bowerbird, Marsh Warbler, and Australian Magpie are known for their ability to mimic other sounds, including the sounds of other bird species, as part of their courtship displays.

Bowing: The male Great Crested Grebe, Hooded Merganser, and Red-capped Manakin bow or strut to display their feathers and attract females.

Flight displays: The Northern Gannet, Red-crowned Crane, Wilson's Snipe, and Manx Shearwater engage in elaborate flight displays to attract mates. During their courtship rituals, they may dive into the water or fly in a zigzagging pattern.

Balancing: The Great Blue Heron, Black-necked Grebe, and Blue-footed Booby use balancing to attract a mate. The Great Blue Heron will stretch out their necks, spread their wings, and be perfectly balanced. The Black-necked Grebe will balance plant materials on their head. The Blue-footed Booby balance their body on one leg to show off a marvelous blue foot.

Bill-clicking: The African Jacana click their bills rapidly to attract a mate. They pair this behavior with wing flapping and singing.

How Do Birds Raise Their Young?

Birds raise their young in a variety of ways depending on the species and their environment. Here are some common ways birds care for their young:

Incubation: Many bird species lay eggs and incubate them until they hatch. During this time, the parents will take turns sitting on the eggs to keep them warm and protect them from predators.

Feeding: Once the eggs hatch, the bird parents feed their young by regurgitating food into their mouths. Their diet can vary depending on the species, but most bird parents will feed their young insects, seeds, or small animals.

Nest-building: Some species build elaborate nests to protect their young from predators and the elements. The parents may use twigs, leaves, and feathers to construct a safe and comfortable nest.

Brooding: After hatching, many bird species will continue to brood their young by keeping them warm and protecting them from predators.

Teaching: As the young birds grow, the parents will teach them how to fly, forage, and avoid predators.

Fledging: Once the young birds are old enough, they leave the nest and fend for themselves. Some species may continue to receive parental care even after leaving the nest.

Aggression: Some bird species, like the American Crow,

will form family groups and engage in cooperative breeding, where non-breeding members of the group help to raise the young by providing food and protection.

What Are Their Feeding Behaviors?

Birds have diverse feeding behaviors to help them survive and thrive. Understanding how they feed themselves can give us further insight into the behavior and ecology of different bird species. This makes the study of bird feeding behaviors an essential aspect of ornithology.

Herbivory: African Grey Parrots, Finches, Hoatzins, and Lorikeets primarily eat plants, including seeds, fruits, berries, and leaves.

Insectivory: Swallows, Flycatchers, and Warblers are insectivorous, meaning they feed primarily on insects and other small arthropods.

Carnivory: Birds of prey, vultures, and penguins are carnivorous and feed on other animals, like fish, rodents, and even other birds.

Omnivory: Mourning Doves, Grackles, European Starlings, and Mallard Ducks have a varied diet that includes both plants and animals.

Seed-cracking: Nuthatches, Sparrows, and Crossbills have unique beaks that allow them to crack open seeds.

Nectar-feeding: Hummingbirds, Sunbirds,

Blossomcrowns, and Sugarbirds feed on nectar.

Scavenging: Vultures, Marabou Storks, Kites, and Caracaras feed on carrion or other dead animals.

Plunge-diving: Gannets and pelicans plunge-dive from great heights to catch fish.

Surface-diving: Ducks and grebes dive below the surface of the water to catch fish or other aquatic animals.

Hovering: Kingfishers and kestrels hover in mid-air while searching for prey.

Pouncing: Falcons and eagles use their speed and agility to pounce on prey from the air.

Wading: Herons and egrets wade through shallow water to catch fish and other aquatic animals.

Probing: Woodpeckers use their beaks to probe into bark or soil to find insects.

Filter-feeding: Flamingos and some ducks filter feed by straining food from water with their beaks.

Kleptoparasitism: Gulls and frigatebirds steal food from other birds.

How Do Birds Communicate?

Birds communicate with each other through a variety of methods. They use vocalizations, visual displays, and physical behaviors. Here are some examples:

Vocalizations: Birds use songs, calls, and other vocalizations to communicate. These sounds can convey a wide range of information, including territorial boundaries, mating calls, and warning signals.

Visual displays: Some bird species use visual displays, like puffing out feathers or displaying colorful plumage, to communicate with each other. These displays can establish dominance, attract mates, or signal aggression.

Physical behaviors: Birds may use physical behaviors, like pecking or nipping, to communicate with each other. For example, some bird species use physical behaviors to establish their place in a social hierarchy.

Chemical signals: Pheromones are chemical signals that can be used to communicate with other birds. This can mark territory, signal reproductive readiness, or establish social bonds.

Dancing: Sage Grouse and other birds engage in elaborate courtship dances that convey information about reproductive fitness and mating readiness.

Mimicry: Parrots and mockingbirds are known for their ability to mimic sounds, including the sounds of other bird species, as a form of communication.

What Are The Different Kinds of Bird Songs?

Bird songs can be categorized into several different types.

Booms: Low, deep vocalizations often used by male bitterns and other birds to attract mates and establish territory.

Caws: Harsh, raucous vocalizations often used by crows and other corvids to communicate with each other and signal danger.

Chirps: Short, high-pitched vocalizations often used in calls to signal alarm or distress.

Clicks: Sharp, clicking vocalizations often used by woodpeckers and other birds to communicate with each other and locate food.

Coos: Doves and pigeons often use soft, gentle vocalizations in**Error! Bookmark not defined.** their courtship displays.

Croaks: Low, deep vocalizations often used by herons and other wading birds to communicate with each other and establish territory.

Gurgles: Low, guttural vocalizations often used by waterfowl and other aquatic birds to communicate with each other and establish territory.

Hoots: Owls and other nocturnal birds often use low-pitched vocalizations to establish territory and communicate with other birds.

Peeps: Chicks and young birds often use soft, high-pitched vocalizations to communicate with their parents.

Rattles: Rapid, staccato vocalizations often used by woodpeckers and other birds to attract mates and establish territory.

Screeches: Raptors and other predatory birds often use high-pitched vocalizations to announce their presence and establish territory.

Trills: Trills are rapidly repeated notes. They add complexity and variation to bird songs.

Trumpets: Loud, trumpet-like vocalizations often used by swans and other large waterfowl to communicate with each other and establish territory.

Warbles: Complex, melodic vocalizations often used in songs to convey information about the bird's quality as a mate.

Whistles: Clear, high-pitched notes often used by songbirds in their songs.

What Do Bird Songs Mean?

Bird songs can have a variety of meanings depending on the species and the context in which they are used. Here are some examples:

Territory establishment: Many bird species use songs to establish and defend their territory from other birds of the same species. The songs can communicate the bird's presence, ownership of the territory, and readiness to defend the area.

Mating: Male birds often use songs to attract a mate during the breeding season. Their songs can communicate the bird's fitness, quality as a potential mate, and availability.

Warning calls: Some bird species use calls to warn other group members or species about potential danger. The calls can alert other birds to the presence of predators or other threats.

Aggression: Birds may use songs to signal aggression or dominance over other birds. This can be important in establishing a hierarchy within a group or species.

Individual identification: Some bird species have unique songs that can be used to identify individuals within the group or species. This can be important for identifying family members or recognizing familiar birds.

Communication: Birds may use songs to communicate with each other about a variety of topics, like the presence of food, the location of a mate, or the location of a nesting site.

Which Birds Are Best At Mimicking Human Speech?

The birds that are best known for mimicking human speech include:

African Grey Parrot

Amazon Parrot

Hill Myna

Indian Ringneck Parakeet

Budgerigar (also known as the common parakeet)

Cockatoo

Eclectus Parrot

Yellow-fronted Canary

Lyrebird

Common Raven

Note that not all individual birds of these species can mimic human speech. Some birds are better at mimicking than others, depending on factors like age, gender, and individual temperament.

3 REMARKABLE AND MEMORABLE BIRDS

Birds are a highly diverse group of animals, with over 10,000 species found throughout the world. They range in size from the tiny bee hummingbird, which weighs less than a penny, to the ostrich, which can reach up to 9 feet tall and weigh over 300 pounds.

Who Are The Smallest Birds?

These birds are known for their tiny size and incredible agility, which allows them to flit through dense vegetation and hover in midair as they feed on nectar or insects.

Bee Hummingbird (2.25 inches / 5.7 cm)

Buff-breasted Pygmy Owl (4 inches / 10 cm)

Goldcrest (3.1 inches / 8 cm)

Least Auklet (5.9 inches / 15 cm)

Spotted Pardalote (3.5 inches / 9 cm)

Willow Warbler (4.3 inches / 11 cm)

Black-capped Chickadee (4.7 inches / 12 cm)

Eurasian Wren (3.7 inches / 9.5 cm)

Ruby-throated Hummingbird (3.5 inches / 9 cm)

Tawny-flanked Prinia (4.7 inches / 12 cm)

Long-tailed Tit (4.7 inches / 12 cm)

Bushtit (3.5 inches / 9 cm)

Gold-ringed Tanager (3.9 inches / 10 cm)

Common Firecrest (3.5 inches / 9 cm)

Pygmy Nuthatch (3.9 inches / 10 cm)

Despite their small size, many of these birds have a high metabolism and require a steady food supply to survive.

Who Are The Largest Birds?

These birds are known for their impressive size and strength, which allows them to hunt, forage, and defend themselves from predators.

Ostrich (up to 9 feet / 2.7 meters tall)

Southern Cassowary (up to 5.6 feet / 1.7 meters tall)

Emu (up to 6.2 feet / 1.9 meters tall)

Great Bustard (up to 4.3 feet / 1.3 meters tall)

Kori Bustard (up to 4.3 feet / 1.3 meters tall)

Somali Ostrich (up to 8.2 feet / 2.5 meters tall)

Andean Condor (up to 4.5 feet / 1.4 meters tall)

California Condor (up to 4.5 feet / 1.4 meters tall)

Dalmatian Pelican (up to 6.2 feet / 1.9 meters tall)

Siberian Crane (up to 5.9 feet / 1.8 meters tall)

Greater Flamingo (up to 5.9 feet / 1.8 meters tall)

Mute Swan (up to 5.6 feet / 1.7 meters tall)

Whooping Crane (up to 5.3 feet / 1.6 meters tall)

Marabou Stork (up to 5.2 feet / 1.6 meters tall)

Trumpeter Swan (up to 5.5 feet / 1.7 meters tall)

Despite their large size, many of these birds are graceful and agile in flight. They have powerful wings and can soar for long distances.

Who Are The Heaviest Birds?

These birds are known for their impressive weight.

Common Ostrich (up to 345 pounds / 156.5 kg)

Somali Ostrich (up to 320 pounds / 145 kg)

Southern Cassowary (up to 167 pounds / 76 kg)

Emu (up to 130 pounds / 59 kg)

Emperor Penguin (up to 99 pounds / 45 kg)

Dalmatian Pelican (up to 33 pounds / 15 kg)

Mute Swan (up to 30 pounds / 13.6 kg)

Whooper Swan (up to 31 pounds / 14 kg)

Trumpeter Swan (up to 28 pounds / 13 kg)

Andean Condor (up to 33 pounds / 15 kg)

California Condor (up to 28 pounds / 13 kg)

Great Bustard (up to 46 pounds / 21 kg)

Kori Bustard (up to 40 pounds / 18 kg)

Indian Peafowl (up to 13 pounds / 6 kg)

Tundra Swan (up to 26 pounds / 12 kg)

The heaviest birds are often flightless or have limited flying abilities, but that isn't strictly true. Flightless the birds like the Emu and Ostrich rely on their strength and agility on the ground to hunt, forage, and defend themselves from predators. The heavy birds that fly, like the condors, can cover 200 miles in a day.

Who Are The Fastest Birds?

These birds are known for their incredible speed and agility, which allows them to hunt and survive in their respective environments.

Peregrine Falcon (up to 240 mph / 386 km/h)

Golden Eagle (up to 200 mph / 320 km/h)
White-throated Needletail (up to 105 mph / 169 km/h)

Gyrfalcon (up to 130 mph / 209 km/h)

Spur-winged Goose (up to 88 mph / 142 km/h)

Eurasian Hobby (up to 100 mph / 161 km/h)

Common Swift (up to 69 mph / 112 km/h)

Red-breasted Merganser (up to 81 mph / 130 km/h)

Frigatebird (up to 95 mph / 153 km/h)

Rock Dove (up to 70 mph / 113 km/h)

Great Snipe (up to 60 mph / 97 km/h)

Mallard (up to 65 mph / 105 km/h)

Anna's Hummingbird (up to 61 mph / 98 km/h)

Northern Gannet (up to 60 mph / 97 km/h)

Common Eider (up to 47 mph / 76 km/h)

It's worth noting that these speeds are estimates based on various sources and can vary depending on a few factors like altitude and wind speed. The individual bird's hunting ability or feeding behavior will also play a part. The speeds listed here are generally for diving or stooping birds, which can achieve higher speeds than birds in level flight.

Which Birds Have the Most Feathers?

These birds are known for their impressive feather count, which plays an important role in their ability to fly, regulate body temperature, and attract mates.

Tundra Swan (25,000 feathers)

American White Pelican (20,000 feathers)

Whooping Crane (20,000 feathers)

Emperor Penguin (18,000 feathers)

Snow Goose (12,000 feathers)

Greater Flamingo (11,000 feathers)

Bar-tailed Godwit (10,000 feathers)

The number of feathers can vary depending on the size and age of the bird. The season and other factors also play a role.

Which Birds Have the Least Feathers?

It's difficult to determine which birds have the least feathers, as most birds have a similar number of feathers relative to their body size. However, some bird species have relatively fewer feathers due to their size or other environmental adaptations.

Hummingbirds: While they are known for their iridescent plumage, hummingbirds have relatively few feathers due to their small size.

Penguins: While they have a dense layer of feathers for insulation, penguins have relatively few feathers overall due to their streamlined body shape.

Emus: Like penguins, emus have a relatively small number of feathers for their large size, which helps them regulate their body temperature in the hot Australian climate.

Kiwis: These flightless birds have a dense layer of feathers, but they have relatively few overall due to their small size and burrowing lifestyle.

Ostriches: While they are among the largest birds in the world, ostriches have relatively few feathers due to their unique body shape and adaptations for running.

Cassowaries: These large, flightless birds have a relatively small number of feathers, which helps them to stay cool in the hot tropical climate.

Bustards: These ground-dwelling birds have relatively few feathers, which helps them to blend in with their surroundings and avoid predators.

Gannets: These diving birds have a streamlined body shape and relatively few feathers, which helps them to move quickly and efficiently through the water.

Herons: While they have a distinctive plumage, herons have relatively few feathers due to their tall, slender body shape.

Ibises: These wading birds have a relatively small number of feathers, which helps them to stay cool in the hot, tropical climate.

Rails: These small, secretive birds have a relatively small number of feathers, which helps them to move quickly and quietly through dense vegetation.

Sandpipers: These shorebirds have a streamlined body shape and relatively few feathers, which helps them to move quickly over sand and mud.

Tinamous: These ground-dwelling birds have relatively few feathers, which helps them to regulate their body temperature in the hot South American climate.

Turacos: These colorful birds have relatively few feathers, which helps them to move quickly and gracefully through the forest canopy.

Woodpeckers: While they have a distinctive plumage, woodpeckers have relatively few feathers due to their slender body shape and adaptations for clinging to trees.

Which Birds Have The Shortest Beaks?

Beak length can vary within a species depending on factors like age, sex, and geographic location. Additionally, the length of a bird's beak can be influenced by its diet and feeding habits, with birds that feed on insects or seeds tending to have shorter beaks than birds that feed on nectar or larger prey. These birds are known for having relatively short beaks compared to other bird species.

Bee Hummingbird (0.6 inches / 1.5 cm)

Goldcrest (0.7 inches / 1.8 cm)

Least Flycatcher (0.4 inches / 1 cm)

Red-breasted Nuthatch (0.7 inches / 1.8 cm)

Black-capped Chickadee (0.5 inches / 1.2 cm)

Common Chiffchaff (0.6 inches / 1.5 cm)

Pygmy Nuthatch (0.6 inches / 1.5 cm)

Eurasian Wren (0.7 inches / 1.8 cm)

Grey Fantail (0.6 inches / 1.5 cm)

Firecrest (0.6 inches / 1.5 cm)

Eurasian Treecreeper (0.6 inches / 1.5 cm)

Willow Warbler (0.6 inches / 1.5 cm)

Yellow-browed Warbler (0.6 inches / 1.5 cm)

Siberian Tit (0.6 inches / 1.5 cm)

Ruby-crowned Kinglet (0.6 inches / 1.5 cm)

Which Birds Have The Longest Beaks?

Beak length can vary within a species depending on factors like age, sex, and geographic location. Additionally, the length of a bird's beak can be influenced by its diet and feeding habits. Birds that feed on insects or seeds tend to have shorter beaks than birds that feed on nectar, fruit, or larger prey. Nonetheless, these birds are known for having relatively long beaks compared to other bird species.

Sword-billed Hummingbird (3.9 inches / 10 cm)

Shoebill (7.9 inches / 20 cm)

Toco Toucan (7.5 inches / 19 cm)

Long-billed Curlew (7.5 inches / 19 cm)

American White Pelican (11.8 inches / 30 cm)

Great Blue Heron (6.0 inches / 15 cm)

American Avocet (3.9 inches / 10 cm)

Brown Pelican (11.0 inches / 28 cm)

Roseate Spoonbill (7.1 inches / 18 cm)

Northern Gannet (4.7 inches / 12 cm)

Atlantic Puffin (1.6 inches / 4 cm)

Black Skimmer (4.7 inches / 12 cm)

Yellow-billed Hornbill (4.1 inches / 10.5 cm)

Keel-billed Toucan (5.9 inches / 15 cm)

Ivory-billed Woodpecker (3.9 inches / 10 cm)

Which Birds Have The Longest Feathers?

Feather length can vary within a species depending on factors like age, sex, and geographic location. The length of a bird's feathers can be influenced by its role in attracting mates or for flight. Birds that engage in elaborate courtship displays or long-distance flights tend to have longer feathers. These birds are known for having relatively long feathers compared to other bird species.

Indian Peafowl (up to 5 feet / 1.5 meters)

Victoria Crowned Pigeon (up to 28 inches / 70 cm)

Greater Bird of Paradise (up to 35 inches / 90 cm)

King Bird of Paradise (up to 16 inches / 40 cm)

Lady Amherst's Pheasant (up to 28 inches / 70 cm)

Marabou Stork (up to 33 inches / 85 cm)

Resplendent Quetzal (up to 28 inches / 70 cm)

Great Argus Pheasant (up to 60 inches / 150 cm)

Andean Condor (up to 14 inches / 35 cm)

Harpy Eagle (up to 19 inches / 48 cm)

Southern Cassowary (up to 10 inches / 25 cm)

Himalayan Monal (up to 18 inches / 45 cm)

Shoebill Stork (up to 12 inches / 30 cm)

White-tailed Tropicbird (up to 18 inches / 45 cm)

White-tailed Eagle (up to 12 inches / 30 cm)

Which Birds Have The Shortest Feet?

Birds have a wide range of foot sizes and shapes that are adapted to their specific lifestyles, so it's difficult to determine which birds truly have the shortest feet. Some bird species have relatively smaller feet due to their small size or adaptations for perching on branches or foraging on the ground. Here are some examples:

Hummingbirds: These small birds have tiny feet that are used for perching on slender branches and flowers.

Kinglets: These small songbirds have short toes that help them cling to small branches and twigs while foraging for insects.

Goldcrests: These tiny birds have slender toes that help them move nimbly through the forest canopy while foraging for insects.

Pygmy Nuthatches: These small birds have short, curved toes that help them cling to tree bark and branches while foraging for insects and seeds.

Eurasian Treecreepers: These small birds have long, curved toes that help them climb up tree trunks while foraging for insects.

Pigeons: While they have relatively large bodies, pigeons have relatively small feet that are used for perching on narrow ledges and branches.

Sparrows: These small songbirds have short toes that help them forage on the ground for seeds and insects.

Wrens: These small, energetic birds have short, sturdy toes that help them move quickly through dense vegetation while foraging for insects.

Kingfishers: These diving birds have relatively small, sharp claws that help them grasp fish and other prey in the water.

Falcons: These birds of prey have relatively small, sharp talons that are used for grasping and killing prey on the ground and in the air.

Sandpipers: These shorebirds have relatively small, slender feet that used for walking on sand and mud.

Ostriches: These large, flightless birds have relatively small feet that are used for running on the ground.

Emus: Like ostriches, emus have relatively small feet that are used for running on the ground.

Cassowaries: These large, flightless birds have relatively small feet that are used for walking and running on the forest floor.

Tinamous: These ground-dwelling birds have relatively small feet that are used for walking and running on the forest floor.

Which Birds Lay The Smallest Eggs?

Egg size can vary within a species depending on factors like age and size of the female. These birds are known for laying relatively small eggs compared to other bird species.

Bee Hummingbird (0.2 inches / 5 mm)

Least Sandpiper (0.9 inches / 23 mm)

Ruby-throated Hummingbird (0.5 inches / 13 mm)

Golden-crowned Kinglet (0.5 inches / 13 mm)

House Wren (0.7 inches / 18 mm)

Common Firecrest (0.5 inches / 12.5 mm)

Willow Warbler (0.6 inches / 15 mm)

Blue-gray Gnatcatcher (0.5 inches / 13 mm)

White-throated Sparrow (0.8 inches / 20 mm)

Yellow Warbler (0.6 inches / 15 mm)

Carolina Wren (0.8 inches / 20 mm)

Song Sparrow (0.8 inches / 20 mm)

Black-capped Chickadee (0.6 inches / 15 mm)

Downy Woodpecker (0.8 inches / 20 mm)

Black-throated Blue Warbler (0.6 inches / 15 mm)

Which Birds Lay The Largest Eggs?

Egg size can vary within a species depending on factors like the age and size of the female. These birds are known for laying relatively large eggs compared to other bird species.

Ostrich (6 x 5 inches / 15 x 13 cm)

Emu (4.7 x 3.5 inches / 12 x 9 cm)

Southern Cassowary (4.5 x 3.5 inches / 11 x 9 cm)

Greater Rhea (4.5 x 3 inches / 11 x 8 cm)

Common Ostrich (4.3 x 3.5 inches / 11 x 9 cm)

Indian Peafowl (2.8 x 2.2 inches / 7 x 5.5 cm)

Emperor Penguin (3.9 x 2.8 inches / 10 x 7 cm)

King Penguin (3.2 x 2.4 inches / 8 x 6 cm)

Southern Rockhopper Penguin (2.5 x 1.8 inches / 6.5 x 4.5 cm)

Gentoo Penguin (3 x 2.2 inches / 7.5 x 5.5 cm)

Northern Royal Albatross (4.7 x 3.2 inches / 12 x 8 cm)

Laysan Albatross (3.5 x 2.5 inches / 9 x 6.5 cm)

Eurasian Oystercatcher (2.8 x 2 inches / 7 x 5 cm)

African Jacana (2.5 x 1.8 inches / 6.5 x 4.5 cm)

Shoebill (3.9 x 3.1 inches / 10 x 8 cm)

Which Birds Have The Most Colorful Feathers?

The coloration of some bird species can vary depending on factors like age, gender, and location. The coloration of some birds may also change depending on the angle and intensity of light hitting their feathers. These birds are known for their striking and colorful plumage.

Peacock: The male peacock has iridescent green and blue feathers with a striking fan-shaped tail of bright blue, green, and gold.

Scarlet Macaw: These birds have bright red, yellow, and blue feathers with a distinctive patch of bare white skin around their eyes.

Resplendent Quetzal: Males have iridescent green and blue feathers, a red breast, and long, trailing tail feathers. Females have similar coloring but without long tail feathers.

Gouldian Finch: These small birds have brightly colored heads with blue, purple, red, and yellow feathers, while their bodies are mostly green or yellow.

Painted Bunting: The male painted bunting has a bright blue head, green back and wings, and a red breast, while the female is mostly green.

Northern Cardinal: The male cardinal has bright red feathers with a black face and mask, while the female is mostly brown with a hint of red on her wings and tail.

Rainbow Lorikeet: These birds have bright green, blue, and red feathers with a distinctive bright blue head and red beak.

Superb Bird-of-Paradise: The male has iridescent green and blue feathers with a striking fan-shaped head crest and long, black tail feathers. The female is mostly brown.

Mandarin Duck: The male has a distinctive orange and brown plumage with a striking white and black striped face, while the female is mostly brown with a hint of orange.

Anna's Hummingbird: These small birds have iridescent green and pink feathers with a bright pink head and throat on the male.

Blue Jay: These birds have striking blue feathers with a distinctive crest on their head and a black collar around their neck.

Golden Pheasant: The male has bright red and gold feathers with a striking crest on his head and long, colorful tail feathers. The female is mostly brown.

Lilac-breasted Roller: These birds have bright blue and green feathers with a striking lilac breast and throat.

Atlantic Puffin: These seabirds have a distinctive orange and black beak with bright orange feet and a white and black body.

Eclectus Parrot: The male has bright green feathers with a red and blue underwing, while the female is mostly red with a blue underwing.

Which Birds Have the Longest Names?

Bird names can vary depending on the authority or organization doing the naming, and some bird species have multiple common names or subspecies with different names. These are some examples of bird species with relatively long scientific names.

Hippolais languida - Upcher's Warbler (found in Europe and Asia)

Pachyramphus homochrous - Bare-crowned Antbird (found in South America)

Psittacella picta - Painted Tiger Parrot (found in New Guinea)

Hemispingus superciliaris - Superciliaried Hemispingus (found in South America)

Galbula chalcothorax - Blue-cheeked Jacamar (found in Central and South America)

Sphyrapicus varius nuchalis - Red-naped Sapsucker (found in North America)

**Cnemophilus macgregorii - MacGregor's Bird-of-

Paradise (found in New Guinea)

Orthotomus derbianus - Chestnut-capped Tailorbird (found in Southeast Asia)

Hemiprocne mystacea - Moustached Treeswift (found in Southeast Asia)

Glaucidium peruanum - Peruvian Pygmy Owl (found in South America)

Malimbus nitens - Gray-headed Malimbe (found in Africa)

Cracticus torquatus leucopterus - White-winged Triller (found in Australia and Papua New Guinea)

Chloropsis cochinchinensis - Blue-winged Leafbird (found in Southeast Asia)

Harpactes orcskios   Sumatran Trogon (found in Southeast Asia)

Chloroceryle amazona stictoptera - Green-and-rufous Kingfisher (found in South America)

4 Winged Inspiration: Birds in Art, Literature, and Entertainment

Bands with Bird Names

There are many musical bands with bird names from all genres of music. The popularity of such band names reflects the enduring fascination and cultural significance of birds in human society.

A Flock of Seagulls

The Penguins

The Byrds

Paul McCartney & Wings

The Partridge Family

Eagles

Counting Crows

The Yardbirds

Sheryl Crow

The O'Jays

The Black Crowes

Old Crow Medicine Show

Eagle-Eye Cherry

Owl City

Taylor Swift

The Sandpipers

The Flamingos

Conway Twitty and The Twittybirds

The Falcons

Robyn

The Housemartins

Famous Bird References in Songs

Birds have been a popular source of inspiration for musicians throughout history. Songs often reference their beauty, freedom, and symbolism. Bird references in music can evoke a wide range of emotions and themes, like love, loss, hope, and transcendence. Whether as a metaphor or a literal subject matter, birds continue to captivate and inspire artists in various genres and styles of music.

"Blackbird singing in the dead of night / Take these broken wings and learn to fly" - Blackbird, The Beatles (1968)

"I'm like a bird, I'll only fly away / I don't know where my soul is, I don't know where my home is" - I'm Like a Bird, Nelly Furtado (2000)

"Birds flying high, you know how I feel / Sun in the sky, you know how I feel" - Feeling Good, Nina Simone (1965)

"Everybody's talking about the bird / Bird, bird, bird, b-bird's the word" - Surfin' Bird, The Trashmen (1963)

"Fly like an eagle / To the sea / Fly like an eagle / Let my spirit carry me" - Fly Like an Eagle, Steve Miller Band (1976)

"Why do we scream at each other?/This is what it sounds like/When doves cry" -When Doves Cry, Prince (1984)

"Rise up this mornin' / Smiled with the risin' sun / Three little birds / Pitch by my doorstep /Singin' sweet songs / Of melodies pure and true / Saying', ("This is my message to you") / Singing' "Don't worry 'bout a thing / 'Cause every little thing gonna be alright." – Three Little Birds, Bob Marley and The Whalers (1977)

"Blue canary in the outlet by the light switch / Who watches over you / Make a little birdhouse in your soul" Build A Little Birdhouse In Your Soul, They Might Be Giants (1990)

"He rocks in the treetops all day long, hoppin' and a-boppin' and singing his song / All the little birds on Jaybird Street love to hear the robin go tweet-tweet-tweet / Rockin' robin, Rock-rock-rockin' robin / Go rockin' robin 'cause we're really gonna rock tonight" Rockin' Robin, Bobby Day (1957)

"Like two sparrows in a hurricane / Trying to find their way / With a head full of dreams /And faith that can move anything" Like Two Sparrows in A Hurricane, Tanya Tucker (1992)

"I hope the eagle takes me / Away from this land / And leaves me where the sky meets the sea" - Landslide, Fleetwood Mac

Bird References in Theatre

Bird references in plays often serve as a symbol of freedom, escape, and change. They contribute to rich and layered meanings that enhance the themes and messages of the works.

The Bluebird by Maurice Maeterlinck (1908) - A play

about a young girl who sets out on a quest to find the bluebird of happiness. The play has been adapted into numerous films, operas, and other works of art.

The Seagull by Anton Chekhov (1895) - A play about a group of artists who spend their summer on a country estate. The title of the play refers to a seagull that is shot by one of the characters.

The Birds by Aristophanes (414 BC) - A play in which two Athenians decide to escape the corruption of the city by building a utopia in the clouds with the help of the birds.

The Swan by Elizabeth Egloff (1989) - A play about a man who is obsessed with a swan that he finds injured on his property. As he cares for the swan, he becomes increasingly detached from reality.

The Owl and the Pussycat by Edward Lear (1871) - A children's play about an owl and a cat who fall in love and run away to get married. The play is based on a poem of the same name.

The Cormorant by Stephen Adly Guirgis (1995) - A play about a man who is released from prison and begins working for his brother, who runs a fish market. The man develops an obsession with a cormorant that he sees swimming in the harbor.

The Birds of Paradise by Richard Brinsley Sheridan (1781) - A play about a group of London socialites vying for the affection of the same woman. The play's title refers to a type of bird known for brightly colored plumage.

Romeo and Juliet by William Shakespeare (1597) – A tragedy about the romance between two Italian youths from feuding families. In it, a lark's singing warns the doomed couple that their time is short.

Birds in Poems

Birds have been a popular subject matter in poetry for centuries. They are often used to symbolize various themes and emotions like freedom, love, hope, and death. From the lark's joyful melodies to the raven's ominous cawing, birds offer poets a rich source of inspiration and imagery. Whether used as metaphors or as literal representations, birds in poetry have the power to evoke a wide range of emotions and meanings that continue to captivate and move readers.

"The Raven" by Edgar Allan Poe (1845) - A poem about a man who is visited by a talking raven. The poem has become one of Poe's most famous works.

"The Waste Land" by T.S. Eliot (1922) - A long, complex poem that references birds throughout, including the nightingale and the crow.

"Ode to a Nightingale" by John Keats (1819) - A poem in which the speaker expresses his desire to escape from the world and join the nightingale in its song.

"When Lilacs Last in the Dooryard Bloom'd" by Walt Whitman (1865) - A poem written in memory of President Abraham Lincoln, which includes references to birds like the hermit thrush and the mockingbird.

"The Wild Swans at Coole" by W.B. Yeats (1917) - A poem in which the speaker reflects on the beauty and majesty of the swans he observes.

"The Eagle" by Alfred, Lord Tennyson (1851) - A poem that describes the power and majesty of the eagle as it soars through the sky.

"The Lark Ascending" by George Meredith (1881) - A poem that captures the beauty and grace of the lark's flight.

"The Windhover" by Gerard Manley Hopkins (1877) - A poem in which the speaker marvels at the beauty and grace of a kestrel in flight.

"Thirteen Ways of Looking at a Blackbird" by Wallace Stevens (1917) - A series of 13 short poems, each describing a different perspective on the blackbird.

"The Bird with the Dark Plumes" by Rabindranath Tagore (1916) - A poem that tells the story of a bird with dark plumes that serves as a metaphor for the power of the human soul.

"The Skylark" by Christina Rossetti (1875) - A poem that celebrates the beauty and song of the skylark.

"Hawk Roosting" by Ted Hughes (1960) - A poem in which the speaker adopts the persona of a hawk and describes the bird's fierce and predatory nature.

Bird in Novels

Bird references in novels often serve as a powerful symbol of freedom, hope, and transformation. Birds in novels offer authors a versatile and evocative symbol that can add depth and complexity to their stories. They also captivate and engage readers.

"To Kill a Mockingbird" by Harper Lee - This classic novel features the mockingbird as a symbol of innocence and the importance of empathy and understanding.

"The Birds" by Daphne du Maurier - This suspenseful horror story features birds that inexplicably begin attacking humans.

"The Maltese Falcon" by Dashiell Hammett - This detective novel features a valuable bird sculpture, the Maltese Falcon, as the central MacGuffin.

"Jonathan Livingston Seagull" by Richard Bach - This allegorical novella tells the story of a seagull's journey to transcendence and self-discovery.

"The Snow Goose" by Paul Gallico - This heartwarming novella tells the story of a man and a young girl who nurse an injured snow goose back to health during World War II.

"The Wild Birds" by Wendell Berry - This novel features the lives and struggles of a family of farmers in rural Kentucky, including their interactions with the birds on their land.

"The Bird Artist" by Howard Norman - This novel tells

the story of a bird artist named Fabian Vas who lives in a remote Canadian fishing village in the early 1900s.

"The Goldfinch" by Donna Tartt - This Pulitzer Prize-winning novel features a stolen painting of a goldfinch as a symbol of the protagonist's lost innocence.

"Treasure Island" by Robert Louis Stevenson - A classic adventure novel about a young boy named Jim Hawkins who sets sail with a group of pirates to find a treasure hidden on a remote island. The Pirate Long John Silver has a talking parrot named Captain Flint.

Bird References in Art

Bird references in works of art have been used for centuries to represent various themes and symbols, like freedom, beauty, and spirituality. Birds have been a popular subject matter for artists across different cultures and time periods. Whether depicted realistically or abstractly, birds in art continue to captivate and inspire viewers with their grace, elegance, and symbolic meanings.

The Goldfinch by Carel Fabritius (1654) - A painting of a pet goldfinch chained to its perch. The painting is currently housed in the collection of the Mauritshuis Museum in The Hague, Netherlands.

The Birds of America by John James Audubon (1827-1838) - A collection of 435 life-sized paintings of birds, including the iconic American flamingo. The collection can be found in the rare books and manuscripts division of the New York Public Library.

Three Studies of a Bird in Flight by Eadweard Muybridge (1885) - A series of photographs that capture the motion of a bird in flight. The photographs can be found in the collection of the Royal Society in London.

The Birds by Salvador Dali (1949) - A surrealist painting that features a flock of birds flying over a desolate landscape. The painting can be found in the collection of the Salvador Dali Museum in St. Petersburg, Florida.

The Owl by Pablo Picasso (1949) - A painting of an owl with large, piercing eyes. The painting can be found in the Museum of Modern Art collection in New York City.

St. Francis in Ecstasy by Giovanni Bellini (1475-1480) - A painting that features a dove perched on the shoulder of St. Francis of Assisi. The painting can be found in the collection of the Frick Collection in New York City.

The Birds by Georges Braque (1960) - A series of paintings that feature abstracted bird forms in bright, bold colors. The paintings can be found in various collections around the world.

The Annunciation by Fra Angelico (1438-1445) - A painting that features the Archangel Gabriel and the Virgin Mary, with a dove representing the Holy Spirit hovering above. The painting can be found in the collection of the San Marco Museum in Florence, Italy.

The Great Wave off Kanagawa by Katsushika Hokusai (1831) - A woodblock print that features a large wave with a group of birds flying above. The print can be found in the Metropolitan Museum of Art collection in New York City.

The Hunters in the Snow by Pieter Bruegel, the Elder (1565) - A painting that features a group of hunters returning from a hunt, with a flock of birds flying overhead. The painting can be found in the collection of the Kunsthistorisches Museum in Vienna, Austria.

The Parakeet and the Mermaid by Henri Matisse (1952) - A cut-out that features a vibrant blue parakeet perched on a branch, with a mermaid swimming in the background. The cut-out can be found in the collection of the Museum of Modern Art in New York City.

The Lady and the Unicorn Tapestries (circa 1500) - A series of six tapestries that feature a unicorn and various birds, including a parrot, a hawk, and a pheasant. The tapestries can be found in the Musée National du Moyen Âge collection in Paris, France.

The Little Owl by William Holman Hunt (1859) - A painting that features a small owl perched on a branch, with the moon visible in the background. The painting can be found in the collection of the Ashmolean Museum in Oxford, England.

The Birds' Party by Giuseppe Arcimboldo (1572) - A painting that features a group of birds arranged to resemble human faces and clothing. The painting can be found in the collection of the Skokloster Castle in Sweden.

Birds in Movies

Bird references in motion pictures have been used to symbolize a variety of themes and emotions, like freedom, beauty, and grace. From the iconic Alfred Hitchcock film "The Birds" to the whimsical animated movie "Rio," birds have been featured prominently in a wide range of films across different genres and styles. Whether used to enhance a storyline, to create a mood, or to simply add visual interest, birds in motion pictures continue to captivate and entertain audiences of all ages.

The Birds directed by Alfred Hitchcock (Universal Pictures, 1963) - A horror movie about a small town that is suddenly attacked by a swarm of birds.

Rio directed by Carlos Saldanha (20th Century Fox, 2011) - An animated movie about a domesticated macaw named Blu who travels to Rio de Janeiro to mate with the last remaining female of his species.

The Owl and the Sparrow directed by Stephane Gauger (Barking Dogs Productions, 2007) - A drama about a young girl who runs away from home and befriends an owl and a sparrow.

Chicken Run directed by Nick Park and Peter Lord (DreamWorks Animation, 2000) - An animated movie about a group of chickens who plot to escape from their farm before they are turned into pies.

Fly Away Home directed by Carroll Ballard (Columbia Pictures, 1996) - A family movie about a young girl who adopts a flock of orphaned geese and teaches them to fly south for the winter.

The Falcon and the Snowman directed by John Schlesinger (Orion Pictures, 1985) - A spy movie about two young men who become involved in espionage and sell information to the Soviet Union.

The Black Swan directed by Darren Aronofsky (Fox Searchlight Pictures, 2010) - A psychological thriller about a ballerina who becomes obsessed with her role as the lead in Swan Lake.

Happy Feet directed by George Miller (Warner Bros. Pictures, 2006) - An animated movie about a young emperor penguin who can't sing but can dance and his journey to find acceptance in his community.

The Eagle directed by Kevin Macdonald (Focus Features, 2011) - A historical drama about a Roman soldier who sets out to retrieve the golden eagle standard of his father's legion.

Birdman directed by Alejandro González Iñárritu (Fox Searchlight Pictures, 2014) - A dark comedy about an aging actor who tries to revive his career by staging a Broadway play.

The Big Year directed by David Frankel (20th Century Fox, 2011) - A comedy about three men who compete to see who can spot the most bird species in a single year.

March of the Penguins directed by Luc Jacquet (Warner Independent Pictures, 2005) - A documentary about the lives of emperor penguins in Antarctica and their journey to mate and raise their young.

Bird Box directed by Susanne Bier (Netflix, 2018) - A horror movie about a woman who must travel blindfolded with her children to avoid supernatural entities.

Dumbo directed by Tim Burton (Walt Disney Studios Motion Pictures, 2019) - A live-action remake of the classic Disney animated movie about a young elephant who can fly. Dumbo is given a "magic feather," which makes him believe he can fly.

Penguin Bloom directed by Glendyn Ivin (Netflix, 2020) - A drama about a family who adopts an injured magpie and how the bird helps them cope with a tragedy.

Birds in Television

Bird references in television have been used to represent a variety of themes and emotions, like love, freedom, and family. From the popular animated series "Tweety and Sylvester" to the award-winning nature documentary "Planet Earth," birds have been featured prominently in a wide range of television programs across different genres and styles. Whether used to educate, to entertain, or to simply add visual interest, birds in television continue to captivate and engage viewers of all ages.

Bird Watching with Farcus and Squawk created by Keith Farcus (PBS, 1997) - A nature show featuring bird expert Keith Farcus and his pet bird, Squawk.

Tweety's High-Flying Adventure directed by James T. Walker (Warner Bros. Animation, 2000) - A direct-to-video animated movie about Tweety Bird and his friends going on a global adventure.

A Bird in the House created by Ellen van Neerven and Gregory J. Brown (ABC iView, 2021) - A short-form digital series featuring five Indigenous Australian writers sharing personal stories about birds and their significance in their culture.

Sesame Street created by Joan Ganz Cooney and Lloyd Morrisett (PBS, 1969) - A children's show featuring a large, yellow bird named Big Bird who lives on Sesame Street.

The Muppet Show created by Jim Henson (ITV, 1976) - A variety show featuring a cast of puppets, including Sam the Eagle and Camilla the Chicken.

The Angry Beavers created by Mitch Schauer (Nickelodeon, 1997) - A cartoon show about two beaver brothers who have wacky adventures, including encounters with a bird named Norbert.

Looney Tunes created by Leon Schlesinger (Warner Bros., 1930) - A series of animated shorts featuring classic characters like Tweety Bird, a small, yellow canary.

Woody Woodpecker created by Walter Lantz (NBC, 1940) - A cartoon show about a zany woodpecker who often gets into trouble.

**Tiny Toon Adventures created by Tom Ruegger (Fox

Kids, 1990) - A cartoon show featuring a group of young animal characters, including Plucky Duck.

DuckTales created by Jymn Magon and Alan Zaslove (Disney Channel, 1987) - A cartoon show about a rich duck named Scrooge McDuck and his family.

Animaniacs created by Tom Ruegger (Fox Kids, 1993) - A cartoon show featuring a cast of zany characters, including a chicken named Chicken Boo.

The Penguins of Madagascar created by Eric Darnell and Tom McGrath (Nickelodeon, 2008) - A cartoon show about a group of penguins who live in the Central Park Zoo and go on wacky adventures.

Birdman and the Galaxy Trio created by Alex Toth (NBC, 1967) - A cartoon show about a superhero named Birdman who fights crime with his powers of flight and strength.

Avian Invasion created by Kevin Burroughs (Animal Planet, 2004) - A documentary series about birds that have invaded cities and towns around the world, and the challenges of dealing with them.

Birds in Comic Books

Bird references in comic books have been used to represent a wide range of themes and emotions, from hope and freedom to darkness and danger. From the iconic Batman villain, The Penguin to the winged superhero Falcon in the Marvel Universe, birds have been a popular subject matter for comic book writers and artists for decades. They have been used as both heroic and villainous characters and have added unique and intriguing dimensions to many comic book storylines.

Batman: The Court of Owls - Owls, DC Comics, 2011 - A storyline in the Batman series that introduces the Court of Owls, a secret society of wealthy Gothamites who use owl imagery in their operations.

Hawkeye - Hawks, Marvel Comics, 2012 - A series focusing on the Marvel superhero Hawkeye, who has a pet hawk named Pizza.

X-Men: Magik - Magpies, Marvel Comics, 1983 - A limited series featuring the character Magik, whose mutant powers allow her to teleport and summon creatures, including magpies.

Birds of Prey - Birds, DC Comics, 1999 - A team-up series featuring female superheroes Black Canary, Oracle, and Huntress, who fight crime in Gotham City.

Buz Sawyer - Eagles, King Features Syndicate, 1943 - A long-running adventure comic strip featuring the character Buz Sawyer, a World War II fighter pilot who encounters eagles during his missions.

The Mighty Thor - Ravens, Marvel Comics, 2012 - A storyline in which the Norse god Thor must confront a group of ravens who have been spying on him.

Spider-Man: The Short Halloween - Vultures, Marvel Comics, 2009 - A Halloween-themed one-shot comic featuring Spider-Man and the villainous Vulture.

Conan the Barbarian - Eagles, Marvel Comics, 1971 - A series featuring the character Conan, a warrior who has an eagle carved on the hilt of his sword.

Animal Man - Birds, DC Comics, 1988 - A series featuring the superhero Animal Man, who gains the powers of animals, including birds.

Wonder Woman: The Circle - Eagles, DC Comics, 2008 - A storyline in which Wonder Woman must battle an eagle-worshipping cult and confront her own past.

The Black Canary - Canaries, DC Comics, 2015 - A limited series focusing on the character Black Canary, who has the ability to unleash powerful sonic screams, which she compares to the songs of canaries.

Samurai Jack - Crows, Cartoon Network, 2001 - A comic book series based on the animated TV show Samurai Jack, in which the titular samurai sometimes battles an army of crows.

Batgirl and the Birds of Prey - Birds, DC Comics, 2016 - A series featuring Batgirl, Black Canary, and Huntress teaming up to take on a criminal organization known as the Blackbirds.

Birds In Fairy Tales

Birds have long been used as symbols in fairy tales, representing everything from freedom and escape to transformation and magic. Birds are also often featured as wise advisors or magical helpers in fairy tales. They can offer guidance, advice, or even magical objects that help the protagonist overcome obstacles and achieve their goals.

Overall, bird references in fairy tales add an element of magic and wonder to these timeless stories and continue to captivate readers of all ages.

The Nightingale - Nightingale, Hans Christian Andersen, Denmark, 1843 - A story in which a Chinese emperor becomes enchanted by the song of a nightingale.

The Ugly Duckling - Ducks, Hans Christian Andersen, Denmark, 1843 - A story in which a young duckling is ostracized for being different, but eventually grows into a beautiful swan.

The Goose Girl - Geese, Brothers Grimm, Germany, 1812 - A story in which a princess is forced to work as a goose girl after being betrayed by her servant.

The Golden Bird - Golden bird, Brothers Grimm, Germany, 1812 - A story in which a prince sets out to capture a golden bird that can grant wishes.

The Firebird - Firebird, Russian fairy tale, Russia, 1910 - A story in which a prince must capture a magical firebird to win the hand of a princess.

The Singing, Springing Lark - Lark, Brothers Grimm, Germany, 1819 - A story in which a princess is turned into a singing lark by her wicked stepmother.

The Swan Maiden - Swans, Scottish fairy tale,

Scotland, 19th century - A story in which a young man falls in love with a swan maiden who can transform between human and swan form.

The White Dove - Dove, Serbian fairy tale, Serbia, 19th century - A story in which a prince must rescue a white dove that has been turned into a beautiful maiden.

The Feather of Finist the Falcon - Falcon, Russian fairy tale, Russia, 19th century - A story in which a young girl falls in love with a prince who is secretly a magical falcon.

The Three Ravens - Ravens, Brothers Grimm, Germany, 1812 - A story in which three ravens tell a grieving mother that they will bring her dead son back to life.

The Blue Bird - Blue Bird, Madame d'Aulnoy, France, 1697 - A story in which two children embark on a magical quest to find the Blue Bird of Happiness.

The Phoenix - Phoenix, Arabian fairy tale, Middle East, 10th century - A story in which a phoenix rises from the ashes of its predecessor, symbolizing rebirth and renewal.

Mythical Birds

Mythical birds have been a part of human culture and folklore for centuries. They often represent divine or supernatural powers. Some of the most famous mythical birds include the phoenix, which symbolizes rebirth and immortality, and the thunderbird, a powerful creature in

Native American mythology associated with thunder and lightning.

Mythical birds can also be found in many other cultures, including the Chinese Fenghuang, the Egyptian Bennu, and the Norse Huginn and Muninn, two ravens associated with the god Odin. These fascinating creatures continue to capture the imagination and inspire artists and storytellers around the world.

Phoenix - A bird from Greek and Egyptian mythology that was said to live for hundreds of years before burning itself up and rising from its own ashes to be reborn.

Roc - A giant bird from Arabic mythology that was said to be able to carry off elephants and other large animals.

Harpy - A bird with the face of a woman from Greek mythology that was said to be the embodiment of storm winds.

Simurgh - A bird from Persian mythology that was said to be so large that it could carry off elephants and entire trees.

Thunderbird - A bird from Native American mythology that was said to create thunder and lightning with its wings. The Thunderbird appears in the mythology of several Native American tribes, including the Ojibwe, the Algonquin, and the Lakota. It continues to be an important symbol in Native American art and culture today.

Garuda - A bird from Hindu mythology that was said to be the mount of the god Vishnu and have the body of a man and the head and wings of an eagle.

Anzu - A bird from Mesopotamian mythology that was said to be so large that it could block out the sun.

Fenghuang - A bird from Chinese mythology that was said to symbolize the five virtues of benevolence, righteousness, propriety, wisdom, and sincerity.

Turul - A bird from Hungarian mythology that was said to be a messenger of the gods and a symbol of power and strength.

Ziz - A giant bird from Jewish mythology that was said to be able to block out the sun with its wings and was associated with the end of the world.

Kinnara - A bird from Hindu and Buddhist mythology that was said to be half-human and half-bird and to possess beautiful singing voices.

Huma bird - A bird from Persian mythology that was said to bring happiness and fortune to those it visited and was said to never land on the ground.

Alkonost - A bird from Slavic mythology that was said to have the head and chest of a woman and the body of a bird, and to have a beautiful singing voice.

Bennu - A bird from Egyptian mythology that was said to represent the sun, creation, and rebirth, and was said to live for 500 years before burning itself up and being reborn.

Sirens - In Greek mythology, the Sirens were said to be half-bird, half-woman creatures whose beautiful singing voices lured sailors to their deaths.

Birds as Pets

Having a bird as a pet can be a rewarding and enjoyable experience for many people. Birds are social animals that can form strong bonds with their owners, and they often have charming personalities and beautiful plumage. Owning a bird also requires a significant amount of time, effort, and resources to ensure its health and well-being. This includes providing a proper diet, adequate living space, and regular veterinary care. It is important to research and understand the needs and behaviors of the species of bird you are considering before bringing one into your home.

Parakeet - A small to medium-sized parrot that is known for its playful personality and ability to mimic sounds.

Canary-winged Parakeet - A small parrot from South America that is known for its affectionate nature and ability to learn tricks.

Bourke's Parrot - A small parrot from Australia that is known for its calm and gentle nature, and for being a relatively quiet bird.

Sun Conure - A small parrot from South America that is known for its vibrant colors and playful personality.

Rosella - A medium-sized parrot from Australia that is known for its striking coloration and playful nature.

Budgerigar (Budgie) - A small parrot from Australia that is known for its playful nature and ability to mimic human speech.

Cockatiel - A small parrot from Australia that is known for its affectionate nature and ability to whistle and mimic sounds.

African Grey Parrot - A medium-sized parrot from Africa that is known for its intelligence and ability to mimic human speech.

Lovebird - A small parrot from Africa that is known for its affectionate nature and strong bond with its owner.

Macaw - A large parrot from South America that is known for its colorful feathers and loud, playful nature.

Cockatoo - A large parrot from Australia that is known for its affectionate nature and ability to mimic sounds.

Canary - A small songbird from the Canary Islands that is known for its melodious singing.

Finch - A small songbird from Africa and Australia that is known for its vibrant colors and lively personality.

Conure - A small to medium-sized parrot from South America that is known for its playful nature and affectionate personality.

Quaker Parrot - A small parrot from South America that is known for its intelligence and ability to mimic human speech.

Amazon Parrot - A medium to large-sized parrot from Central and South America known for its colorful feathers and playful personality.

Pionus Parrot - A medium-sized parrot from Central and South America that is known for its calm, gentle nature.

Eclectus Parrot - A medium-sized parrot from the Pacific Islands that is known for its striking coloration and ability to mimic sounds.

Senegal Parrot - A small parrot from West Africa that is known for its intelligence and affectionate personality.

5 Wandering with Wings: Bird Watching and Appreciation

Who Studies Birds?

Ornithologist: This is a scientist who specializes in the study of birds, including their behavior, biology, and ecology.

Avian ecologist: This is a scientist who studies the relationships between birds and their environment, including the impacts of human activity on bird populations.

Birdwatcher: This is a person who enjoys observing and identifying birds in their natural habitat, either as a hobby or for scientific purposes.

Bird bander: This is a person who attaches small metal bands to the legs of birds to track their movements and study their behavior.

Bird photographer: This is a person who specializes in taking photographs of birds, often for artistic or scientific purposes.

Bird artist: This is a person who creates artwork featuring birds, either for artistic or scientific purposes.

Bird conservationist: This is a person who works to protect and preserve bird populations and their habitats, often through advocacy, education, or direct action.

Bird rehabilitator: This is a person who cares for injured or orphaned birds, with the goal of returning them to the wild once they are healthy enough to survive.

John James Audubon

John James Audubon was a French American ornithologist, naturalist, and artist who lived from 1785 to 1851.

Audubon is best known for his book "The Birds of America," which contains over 400 life-size illustrations of North American birds.

Audubon was born in Haiti and grew up in France before emigrating to the United States as a young man.

Audubon spent much of his life traveling across North America, studying and drawing the region's bird species.

Audubon's illustrations of birds are renowned for their accuracy and attention to detail. They are still widely admired today.

Audubon was a self-taught artist who developed his own unique style of painting and drawing.

Audubon was a passionate conservationist who advocated for the protection of birds and their habitats and was one of the first people to recognize the importance of the natural world for human well-being.

Audubon's work inspired George Bird Grinnell, who founded the **National Audubon Society** in 1905. It is now one of the largest and most respected environmental organizations in the world.

Audubon was also an accomplished musician and composer. He played the flute and violin.

Audubon's passion for bird watching and nature was sparked at a young age, when he discovered a dead oriole and was captivated by its beauty.

Audubon was a skilled hunter and spent many years collecting bird specimens for his illustrations, often shooting them himself.

Audubon's illustrations of birds are still considered some of the most beautiful and accurate depictions of North American birds ever created.

In addition to his bird illustrations, Audubon also created a series of paintings depicting the life of the Native Americans based on his own experiences living among Native American tribes.

Audubon's legacy continues to inspire people today, and his name has become synonymous with bird conservation and appreciation.

John James Audubon's son, **John Woodhouse Audubon**, followed in his father's footsteps. He became a naturalist, writer, and painter. He and his brother, Victor, worked together to have their father's work published.

George Bird Grinnell

George Bird Grinnell (1849-1938) was an American anthropologist, historian, naturalist, and conservationist. Here are some interesting facts about him:

Grinnell was born in Brooklyn, New York, in 1849. As a child, he and his brothers and sisters attended a school taught by **Lucy Audubon**, the wife the John James Audubon. After that, he spent the rest of his youth in the Midwest. He attended Yale University, where he studied under famous naturalist Othniel C. Marsh.

Grinnell was one of the founders of the **Audubon Society**, which he helped to establish in 1905.

He was also a co-founder of the **Boone and Crockett Club**, a conservation organization focused on the protection of big game species in North America. **Theodore Roosevelt** was also a founding member of the club.

Grinnell was also an important figure in the early history of Yellowstone National Park and played a key role in its establishment as the first national park in the United States. He served as the park's first official historian and helped to develop many of the park's early policies and management practices.

Grinnell died in 1938 at the age of 89, but his legacy lives on through his numerous contributions to the fields of conservation, anthropology, and natural history.

The Audubon Society

The **Audubon Society** is a non-profit environmental organization dedicated to the conservation and protection of birds and their habitats.

The society was founded in 1905 by a group of bird enthusiasts led by **George Bird Grinnell** with the goal of promoting the conservation of wild birds and their habitats.

The society is named after **John James Audubon**, a French American artist and naturalist who is widely regarded as one of the greatest bird illustrators of all time.

Today, the **National Audubon Society** is one of the largest and most respected environmental organizations in the world, with over 2.5 million members and supporters.

The society operates over 450 bird sanctuaries and nature centers across the United States, as well as several international conservation programs.

The society is actively involved in research, education, and advocacy on a wide range of bird conservation issues, including habitat protection, bird migration, and climate change.

The society's annual **Christmas Bird Count**, which began

in 1901, is one of the longest-running citizen science projects in the world and provides valuable data on bird populations and distribution.

The society also publishes a few magazines, including **"Audubon,"** which is widely regarded as one of the premier birding magazines in the world.

In recent years, the society has increasingly focused on engaging with diverse communities and promoting social and environmental justice, recognizing that conservation efforts must be inclusive and equitable to be successful.

The society played a key role in the passage of the **Migratory Bird Treaty Act of 1918**, which protects migratory birds and their habitats in the United States.

The society has a strong tradition of engaging young people in bird conservation and environmental education with programs like the **Audubon Adventures classroom program** and the **Audubon Youth Leaders program**.

The society operates several online tools and resources to help birders and nature enthusiasts identify and learn about bird species, including the **Audubon Bird Guide** app and the **eBird database**.

The society has been involved in several high-profile legal battles over environmental issues, including a successful lawsuit in the United States against the efforts to roll back protections for migratory birds.

The society has a strong network of chapters and affiliates across the United States, as well as partnerships with numerous other environmental organizations and government agencies, allowing it to have a broad impact on bird conservation and environmental protection.

About Bird Watching

Bird watching is one of the most popular hobbies in the world, with millions of people participating every year.

The United States has the largest number of bird watchers, with over 45 million people enjoying the activity.

The earliest recorded bird watcher is believed to be Englishman **Gilbert White**, who lived from 1720 to 1793. White was a naturalist and author who is best known for his book "The Natural History and Antiquities of Selborne," which chronicles the flora and fauna of his hometown in Hampshire, England. In his book, White provides detailed observations of local birds and their behavior, and he is often credited as being one of the first people to engage in the scientific study of birds.

Bird watching is a great way to connect with nature and enjoy the beauty of the outdoors.

Bird watchers often use binoculars and telescopes to get a closer look at birds, and many also use field guides to help them identify different species.

Bird watching can be done anywhere in the world, from the middle of a city to the depths of a jungle.

Bird watchers often participate in bird counts and surveys to help track bird populations and monitor changes in their behavior.

Many bird watchers also participate in conservation efforts to protect bird habitats and prevent species from becoming endangered.

Some bird watchers keep a "life list" of all the bird species they have observed in their lifetime.

Bird watching is a great activity for people of all ages and can be a wonderful way to spend time with family and friends while enjoying the natural world.

Tools For Bird Watching

You don't need much to get started with bird watching. Here are some tools that can help you make the most of your bird watching experience:

Binoculars - A good pair of binoculars is the most important tool for bird watching. Look for binoculars that have a magnification of at least 7x and an objective lens diameter of 35mm or more.

Field Guide - A field guide to birds is essential for identifying the birds you see. Choose a guide that is specific to your region and has clear illustrations or photographs.

Notebook - A notebook can be useful for recording your bird sightings, as well as notes on behavior, habitat, and other details.

Birding App - A birding app on your phone can be helpful for identifying birds in the field, as well as keeping track of your sightings.

Clothing - Wear comfortable clothing that is appropriate for the weather, including sturdy shoes or boots.

Hat and Sunscreen - Protect yourself from the sun by wearing a hat and applying sunscreen.

Water and Snacks - Bring water and snacks to stay hydrated and energized during your adventure.

Camera - A camera can be useful for taking photos of birds you see, as well as recording details that can help with identification.

Bird Feeder - If you plan to watch birds from your own backyard, consider setting up a bird feeder to attract a variety of species.

Birdhouse - A birdhouse can also be a great addition to your backyard bird watching setup, as it can provide nesting opportunities for birds in your area.

Tips For Bird Watching

Start with a good pair of binoculars – this is the most important tool for bird watching.

Choose a spot with a diverse range of habitats, like a forest edge or wetland area.

Look for birds at dawn or dusk when they are most active.

Listen for bird calls and songs – this can be just as important as visual identification.

Keep a bird identification guide handy and learn to use it quickly.

Practice patience and take your time to observe and identify birds.

Dress appropriately for the weather and wear comfortable shoes.

Be quiet and move slowly to avoid startling birds.

Use a tripod or other stabilizing device to keep your binoculars steady.

Keep a record of the birds you see and the date and location of your sightings.

Use a notebook or birding app to take notes on behavior, habitat, and other details.

Watch for movement – even the slightest twitch can give away a bird's location.

Watch for patterns of behavior – some birds have distinct flight patterns or feeding behaviors.

Pay attention to color and markings – these can help you identify different species.

Look for birds in pairs or groups – many birds are social and travel in flocks.

Watch for birds of prey, which often perch in trees or on high perches.

Use your ears – birds are often easier to hear than to see, especially in dense foliage.

Look for birds near water sources – many birds are attracted to rivers, lakes, and wetlands.

Respect the birds and their habitats – avoid disturbing nesting areas or sensitive habitats.

Share your love of bird watching with others – it's a great way to introduce people to the wonders of the natural world.

Best Locations for Bird Watching

The best locations for bird watching can vary depending on where you live and the types of birds you want to see. However, here are some general locations that are often great for bird watching:

National Parks and Wildlife Refuges - These protected areas often have diverse habitats that attract a wide range of bird species.

Wetlands and Marshes - These habitats are especially good for waterfowl and wading birds, like herons and egrets.

Forests and Woodlands - These habitats are home to a variety of songbirds, woodpeckers, and raptors.

Coastal Areas - Coastal habitats like beaches and rocky shores can be great places to see seabirds and shorebirds.

City Parks and Gardens - Urban areas can also offer great bird watching opportunities, especially in parks and gardens with diverse plantings that attract a variety of bird species.

Nature Reserves and Sanctuaries - These protected areas are often managed specifically for wildlife, making them excellent locations for bird watching.

Birding Festivals - Many cities and towns hold birding festivals that offer guided tours, workshops, and other opportunities to see a variety of bird species.

Your Own Backyard - Don't overlook the potential for bird watching in your own backyard! Set up a bird feeder or bird bath to attract birds to your yard, and keep a pair of binoculars handy for close-up views.

More Fun Facts About Bird Watching

Bird watching is one of the fastest-growing hobbies in the world, with millions of enthusiasts worldwide.

The world record for the most bird species seen in a single year is over 6,000 species!

The term "birdwatching" is more commonly used in the UK,

while "birding" is more common in the US.

Some bird watchers keep "life lists" of all the bird species they have ever seen.

The **American Birding Association** was founded in 1968 to promote bird watching and conservation.

The Cornell Lab of Ornithology's **eBird** website allows bird watchers to track their sightings and contribute to citizen science research.

Some bird watchers participate in "Big Day" events, where they try to see as many bird species as possible in a single day.

The famous ornithologist and bird artist John James Audubon is considered one of the pioneers of bird watching.

Many bird watchers use smartphone apps to identify birds they see in the field.

"Chasing" rare bird species is a common pursuit among serious bird watchers.

Bird watching can be a great way to connect with nature and reduce stress and anxiety.

Some bird watchers travel the world to see rare and exotic bird species in their natural habitats.

Bird watching can be a great activity for families to enjoy together.

Some bird watchers specialize in a particular group of birds, like raptors or waterfowl.

Bird watching can inspire a deeper appreciation and understanding of the natural world and the importance of conservation efforts.

Are You Interested In Bird Watching?

If you are interested in bird watching, there are many things you can do to get started:

Get some basic equipment - You'll need a pair of binoculars and a field guide to help you identify birds. You can also invest in a spotting scope or camera if you want to take your birding to the next level.

Find a good birding location - Look for parks, nature reserves, and other areas where birds are known to congregate. Local birding groups and online forums can also be helpful for finding good spots in your area.

Join a birding club or organization - This can be a great way to meet other bird enthusiasts and learn more about birds. Many birding groups organize trips and events, which can provide opportunities to see new bird species and learn new skills.

Participate in citizen science projects - There are many citizen science projects that rely on data collected by bird watchers. By participating in these projects, you can help scientists track bird populations and migration patterns.

Attend birding festivals and events - Many cities and towns hold birding festivals and events, which can provide opportunities to see rare or unusual bird species, attend bird-related talks and workshops, and meet other bird enthusiasts.

Keep a birding journal - Keeping a journal of your birding experiences can be a great way to track your progress, record your sightings, and reflect on your experiences.

Learn about bird conservation - Birds face many threats, including habitat loss, climate change, and pollution. Learning about these threats and what can be done to protect birds can be a rewarding and important part of bird watching.

Remember, bird watching is a lifelong learning process, and there's always more to discover and learn about birds. Enjoy the journey!

Bird Conservation

Birds play a crucial role in maintaining ecosystem balance and biodiversity.

According to the International Union for Conservation of Nature (IUCN), over 1,500 bird species are currently threatened with extinction.

The primary threats to bird populations include habitat loss, pollution, climate change, hunting, and illegal trade.

Many organizations, like the Audubon Society, **BirdLife International**, and the **Cornell Lab of Ornithology**, are dedicated to bird conservation efforts around the world.

Some bird conservation efforts include habitat restoration, captive breeding programs, and public education and awareness campaigns.

The **Migratory Bird Treaty Act,** enacted in 1918, protects migratory bird species from hunting and other forms of harm in the United States.

The **Endangered Species Act** enacted in 1973, provides protections for endangered and threatened species, including many bird species.

Many bird species, like the Bald Eagle and the Peregrine Falcon, have made a remarkable recovery due to conservation efforts.

Conservation efforts can benefit not only bird populations but also other wildlife and their habitats.

Citizen science programs, like the Christmas Bird Count and eBird, allow bird watchers to contribute to conservation efforts by collecting data on bird populations and distribution.

Why Are Birds Important to Our Ecosystem?

Birds play a vital role in our ecosystem and are important indicators of the health of our planet.

Pollination: Many birds feed on nectar and pollen, and as they move from flower to flower, they transfer pollen on their beaks and bodies. Their manure is a natural fertilizer. This process is critical for plant reproduction and helps to maintain biodiversity.

Pest control: Birds also help to control insect and rodent populations, which can otherwise cause damage to crops and spread diseases.

Seed Scattering: Some bird species, like frugivores, feed on fruit and scatter, or disperse, seeds throughout their range. This helps to maintain plant diversity and support the growth of new vegetation.

Nutrient cycling: Nutrient cycling refers to the process by which nutrients like carbon, nitrogen, and phosphorus are transferred between living organisms and the environment. As birds feed and defecate, they contribute to the nutrient cycling in their ecosystems. Bird droppings are rich in nitrogen, phosphorus, and other essential nutrients, which can improve soil fertility.

Ecotourism: Bird watching is a popular hobby and can generate significant revenue for local communities. This helps to support conservation efforts and promote sustainable development. While exact figures are difficult to determine, it is estimated that ecotourism contributes billions of dollars to the global economy each year. According to the United Nations World Tourism Organization, ecotourism accounts for 7% of the world's tourism market, and the market share is growing.

Signs of environmental health: Birds are sensitive to

changes in their environment and can serve as indicators of habitat loss, pollution, and other threats to biodiversity. Monitoring bird populations can help us to identify and address these issues before they become more widespread.

Birds are critical to the functioning of our ecosystems. Their conservation is essential for the well-being of our planet and all its inhabitants.

Thank You

Thanks for reading! As we come to the end of this book on bird trivia, I hope you have gained a greater appreciation for the incredible world of birds. Whether you are a well-seasoned birder or just starting out, there is always more to discover and learn about these fascinating creatures.

Through fun feathered facts on bird behavior, anatomy, and ecology, we learn more about the important role that birds play in our environment and in our human culture. From their beautiful songs and stunning plumage to their incredible migratory journeys and complex social behaviors, birds continue to captivate us and inspire us in countless ways.

As you continue your own bird adventures, remember to keep your eyes and ears open. Approach every sighting with curiosity and respect. Whether you are observing a common backyard bird or a rare and elusive species, each bird has a unique story to tell and a vital place in our natural world.

So go forth with your binoculars, your field guide, and your sense of wonder, and let the world of birds continue to amaze and inspire you for years to come. Happy birding!

REFERENCES AND SOURCES

There are many resources available for someone who wants to learn more about birds. One great place to start is at your local library, which will have many books on bird identification, behavior, and conservation. Online resources, like the websites of birding organizations like the Audubon Society and the Cornell Lab of Ornithology, also offer a wealth of information on birding and bird conservation. Here are a few I used to get you started:

"The Backyard Birdwatcher's Bible Birds, Behaviors, Habitats, Identification, Art & Other Home Crafts" by Paul Sterry

"The Big Year: A Tale of Man, Nature, and Fowl Obsession" by Mark Obmascik

"Bird Sense: What It's Like to Be a Bird" by Tim Birkhead

"The Bird Watching Answer Book" by Laura Erickson

"The Bird Watching Handbook: A Guide to the Natural History of the Birds of Britain and Europe" by Paul Sterry

"Birding Without Borders: An Obsession, a Quest, and the Biggest Year in the World" by Noah Strycker

"Birds" by Tim Flach

"Birds of America" by Lorrie Moore

"The Cornell Lab of Ornithology Handbook of Bird Biology" by Irby J. Lovette and John W. Fitzpatrick

"The Crossley ID Guide: Eastern Birds" by Richard Crossley

"The Genius of Birds" by Jennifer Ackerman

"The Handbook of Bird Identification: For Europe and the Western Palearctic" by Mark Beaman and Steve Madge

"The Life of Birds" by David Attenborough

"The Migration of Birds: Seasons on the Wing" by Janice M. Hughes

"National Geographic Field Guide to the Birds of North America" by Jon L. Dunn and Jonathan Alderfer

"Peterson Field Guide to Birds of North America" by Roger Tory Peterson

"The Sibley Guide to Birds" by David Allen Sibley

"The Warbler Guide" by Tom Stephenson and Scott Whittle

"What It's Like to Be a Bird "From Flying to Nesting, Eating to Singing-What Birds Are Doing, and Why" by David Allen Sibley

Attending birding festivals and events can provide opportunities to learn from experts and connect with other bird enthusiasts. Also, joining a local birding club or group can be a great way to get involved in birding and connect with others who share your passion for birds.

Index

adaptations, 35, 36, 40
African Grey Parrot, 27, 71
African Grey Parrots, 21
African Jacana, 44
African Palm Swifts, 17
aggression, 23
Aggression, 14, 20, 26
'Alala, 8
Alan Zaslove, 63
Albatross, 43
albatrosses, 7
Alex Toth, 63
Alfred Hitchcock, 59
Alfred, Lord Tennyson, 54
Alkonost, 69
Altitudinal migration, 15
Amazon Parrot, 27, 72
American Avocet, 38
American Birding Association, 85
American Crows, 16
American Oystercatcher, 16
American Robin, 11, 14
American Robins, 17
American White Pelican, 33, 38
anatomy, viii, 3, 91
Andean Condor, 15, 30, 31, 39
Animal Man, 65
Anna's Hummingbird, 33, 45
Antarctic, 6
Antarctica, 5, 6, 61
Anzu, 69
Arctic, 6
Arctic Tern, 15
Aristophanes, 52
Asia, 9, 10, 11, 12, 46, 47
Atlantic Puffin, 38, 45
Atlantic Puffins, 17
Audubon, 56, 74, 75, 76, 77, 78, 85, 88, 92
Audubon Bird Guide, 78
Australia, 10, 47, 70, 71
Avian ecologist, 73
backyard, 81, 84, 91
Bald eagles, 17
Baltimore Oriole, 17
Bare-crowned Antbird, 46
Barn Swallow, 11
Bar-tailed Godwit, 34
Bar-tailed Godwit,, 15
Bathing, 14
Baya Weaver, 17
beaks, 1, 2, 3, 6, 22, 36, 37
Bee Hummingbird, 28, 36, 42
behaviors, viii, 13, 14, 18, 21, 23, 70, 82, 91
Bennu, 68, 69
Big Bird, 62
binoculars, 79, 80, 81, 82, 84, 86, 91

Bird bander, 73
bird counts, 79
bird feeder, 81, 84
Bird of Paradise, 39
Bird photographer, 73
bird watcher, viii, 79
Bird watching, 79, 80, 84, 85, 86, 89
birdhouse, 81
Birding App, 81
Birding Festivals, 84
BirdLife International, 88
Birdman, 60, 63
Bird-of-Paradise, 45, 47
Birds of Paradise, 52
birds of prey, 6, 12, 41, 83
Birds of prey, 6, 21
Birdwatcher, 73, 92
Black Skimmer, 38
Black Stilt, 9
blackbird, 54
Black-capped Chickadee, 15, 29, 36, 42
Black-throated Blue Warbler, 42
Blossomcrowns, 22
Blue Bird, 67
Blue Jay, 45
Blue Jays, 15
Bluebird, 52
Bluebirds, 16
Blue-cheeked Jacamar, 46
Blue-gray Gnatcatcher, 42
Blue-throated Macaw, 9
Blue-winged Leafbird, 47
Bob Marley, 51
Bobby Day, 51
Bohemian Waxwing, 15
bones, 3

Booms, 24
Boone and Crockett Club, 76
Bourke's Parrot, 70
Bowerbird, 18
brood, 20
Brothers Grimm, 66, 67
Budgerigar, 27, 70
Buff-breasted Pygmy Owl, 28
Burrowing Owls, 17
Bushtit, 29
Bustards, 35
Byrds, 48
California Condor, 30, 31
canary, 51, 62
Canary, 64, 65, 70, 71
Captain Flint, 56
Caracaras, 22
Carel Fabritius, 56
carnivorous, 1, 21
Carolina Wren, 42
Carroll Ballard, 59
Cartoon Network, 65
Cassowaries, 35, 41
Caws, 24
Cedar Waxings, 16
Cedar Waxwing, 15
chemical signals, 23
Chestnut-capped Tailorbird, 47
Chickadees, 16
chicken, 63
Chicken, 7, 59, 62, 63
Chiffchaff, 30
Chirps, 24
Christina Rossetti, 54
Christmas Bird Count, 77, 88
city pigeon, 11

Clicks, 24
climate change, 8, 77, 87
Coastal, 84
Cockatoo, 27, 71
Common Blackbird, 11
Common Crossbill, 15
Common Eider, 33
Common Firecrest, 29, 42
Common Kestrel, 12
common pigeon, 11
communicate, 14, 23, 24, 25, 26
communication, 23
condors, 32
conservation, viii, 75, 76, 77, 78, 79, 80, 85, 86, 87, 88, 89, 90, 92
conservationist, 74, 75, 76
Conure, 71
Coos, 24
Coots, 17
cormorant, 52
Cormorant, 52
cormorants, 7, 14
Cornell Lab of Ornithology, 85, 88, 92
courtship, viii, 14, 18, 19, 23, 24, 38
courtship rituals, viii, 14
Crested Auklets, 17
Croaks, 24
crop, 4
Crossbills, 21
crow, 53
Crow, 8, 20, 49
Crowes, 49
crows, 24, 65
Crows, 49, 65
Dalmatian Pelican, 30, 31
dances, 18, 23

Daphne du Maurier, 55
Dashiell Hammett, 55
David Allen Sibley, 93
David Attenborough, 93
DC Comics, 64, 65
desert, 5, 6
deserts, 1, 5, 6
diet, 2, 3, 20, 21, 36, 37, 70
diving, 22, 33, 35, 41
dominance, 23
Donna Tartt, 56
dove, 57, 67
doves, 50
Downy Woodpecker, 42
duck, 8, 9, 11, 63
Duck, 8, 45, 63
duckling, 66
ducks, 7, 22
Eadweard Muybridge, 57
eagle, 50, 51, 54, 60, 65, 68
Eagle, 9, 39, 49, 50, 54, 60, 62, 88
eagles, 1, 6, 22, 64
Eagles, 48, 64, 65
eBird, 78, 85, 88
eBird database, 78
Eclectus Parrot, 27, 46, 72
Ecotourism, 89
Edgar Allan Poe, 53
eggs, 1, 2, 7, 20, 42, 43
egrets, 22
Ellen van Neerven, 62
Emperor Penguin, 31, 33, 43
Emu, 30, 31, 32, 43
emus, 7
Emus, 34, 41
endangered, 8, 9, 10, 80, 88
Endangered Species Act, 88

Eric Darnell, 63
estuaries, 4
Eurasia, 10
Eurasian Hobby, 32
Eurasian Wigeon, 15
Eurasian Wren, 29, 37
Europe, 8, 10, 11, 12, 46, 92, 93
European Bee-eater, 17
European Starling, 10
European Starlings, 21
Falcon, 55, 60, 63, 67
falcons, 6, 22
Falcons, 41, 49
feathers, 1, 2, 3, 13, 14, 17, 18, 19, 20, 23, 33, 34, 35, 36, 38, 44, 45, 46, 71, 72
Fenghuang, 68, 69
filter feed, 22
Finch, 71
Finches, 21
firebird, 66
Firecrest, 37
Fish Eagle, 9
flamingos, 22
Flamingos, 49
Fleetwood Mac, 51
flight, 1, 2, 3, 19, 30, 33, 38, 54, 57, 63, 82
Flightless, 7
Flycatcher, 36
Flycatchers, 21
Foraging, 13
forests, 4
Forests, 4, 84
Fra Angelico, 57
Frigatebird, 32
frigatebirds, 22
gannets, 22
Gannets, 35

Gardens, 84
Garuda, 68
geese, 7, 59
Gentoo Penguin, 43
George Bird Grinnell, 75, 76, 77
Georges Braque, 57
Gerard Manley Hopkins, 54
gifts, 18
Gilbert White, 79
Giovanni Bellini, 57
Giuseppe Arcimboldo, 58
gizzard, 4
Glendyn Ivin, 61
Goldcrest, 28, 36
Goldcrests, 40
Golden bird, 66
Golden Eagle, 15, 32
Golden-crowned Kinglet, 42
goldfinch, 56
Gold-ringed Tanager, 29
goose, 6, 55, 66
Goose, 8, 32, 33, 55, 66
Gouldian Finch, 44
Grackles, 21
grasslands, 4
Gray-headed Malimbe, 47
Great Blue Heron, 38
Great Bustard, 30, 31
Great Indian Bustard, 9
Great Snipe, 33
Greater Flamingo, 30, 34
grebes, 22
Green-and-rufous Kingfisher, 47
Gregory J. Brown, 62
Grey Fantail, 37
Grey-rumped Treeswifts, 17

Grinnell, vi, 76, 77
gulls, 7, 22
Gurgles, 24
Gyrfalcon, 32
habitat loss, 8, 9, 10, 87, 90
Hans Christian Andersen, 66
Harper Lee, 55
Harpy, 39, 68
Hawaiian Crow, 8
hawk, 54, 58, 64
hawks, 1, 6
Hawks, 17, 64
heart, 2, 3, 4
Helmeted Hornbill, 10
Henri Matisse, 58
Herbivory, 21
hermit thrush, 53
herons, 22, 24, 35, 83
Herons, 35
High-altitude peaks, 5
Hill Myna, 27
Himalayan Monal, 39
Himalayas, 6
Hoatzins, 21
Hoots, 24
House Finches, 17
House Sparrow, 10
House Wren, 42
Housemartins, 49
Howard Norman, 55
Huginn, 68
Huma bird, 69
hummingbirds, 1, 22, 34
Hummingbirds, 7, 21, 34, 40
hunting, 8, 9, 33, 87, 88
Ibises, 35
incubate, 20
Indian Peafowl, 31, 39, 43
Indian Ringneck

Parakeet, 27
Insectivory, 21
Irby J. Lovette, 92
Ivory-billed Woodpecker, 38
Jacanas, 17
James T. Walker, 62
Janice M. Hughes, 93
Jennifer Ackerman, 93
Jim Henson, 62
Joan Ganz Cooney, 62
John James Audubon, 76
John Keats, 53
John W. Fitzpatrick, 92
Jon L. Dunn, 93
Jonathan Alderfer, 93
Jymn Magon, 63
Katsushika Hokusai, 57
Keel-billed Toucan, 38
Keith Farcus, 61
kestrel, 54
kestrels, 22
Kevin Burroughs, 63
Kevin Macdonald, 60
Killdeer, 16
King Features Syndicate, 64
King Penguin, 43
kingfishers, 17, 22
Kingfishers, 41
Kinglets, 40
Kinnara, 69
Kites, 22
kiwis, 7
Kiwis, 34
Kleptoparasitism, 22
Kori Bustard, 30, 31
Lapland Longspur, 15
Lark, 54, 66
Laura Erickson, 92

Least Auklet, 28
Leon Schlesinger, 62
Lilac-breasted Roller, 45
Lloyd Morrisett, 62
Long-billed Curlew, 37
Long-tailed Tit, 29
Lorikeets, 21
Lorrie Moore, 92
Lovebird, 71
Luc Jacquet, 60
Lyrebird, 27
Macaw, 71
Madagascar, 9, 63
Madagascar Pochard, 9
Madame d'Aulnoy, 67
magpies, 64
Mallard, 11, 33
Mallard Ducks, 21
Maltese Falcon, 55
Marabou Stork, 30, 39
Marabou Storks, 22
Mark Beaman, 93
Mark Obmascik, 92
marshes, 4
Marshes, 83
Marvel Comics, 64, 65
mating, 13, 23
migration, 14, 15, 16, 77, 86
Migration, 13, 14, 93
Migratory Bird Treaty, 78
Migratory Bird Treaty Act,, 88
mimic, viii, 19, 23, 70, 71, 72
mimicking, 27
Mitch Schauer, 62
mockingbird, 53, 55
Moorhens, 17
mountains, 1
Mourning Doves, 21
Moustached Treeswift, 47

Muninn, 68
Mute Swan, 30, 31
National Audubon Society, 75, 77
National Parks, 83
nectar, 1, 7, 28, 36, 37, 89
Nelly Furtado, 50
nesting, 16, 17, 26, 81, 83
nests, 13, 14, 16, 17, 18, 20
New Zealand, 9
nightingale, 53, 66
Nightingale, 53, 66
Nina Simone, 50
Noah Strycker, 92
Norbert, 62
North America, 7, 10, 11, 46, 74, 76, 93
Northern Cardinal, 45
Northern Cardinals, 15
Northern Gannet, 33, 38
Northern Lapwings, 16
Nuthatches, 21
oceans, 1, 4, 5
O'Jays, 49
Omnivory, 21
Ornithologist, 73
ornithology, 21
Osprey, 17
Ospry, 15
Ostrich, 29, 30, 31, 32, 43
ostriches, 7
Ostriches, 34, 41
owl, 5, 52, 57, 58, 59, 64
Owl, 49, 52, 57, 58, 59
owls, 6
Oystercatcher, 43
Pablo Picasso, 57
Painted Bunting, 44
Painted Tiger Parrot, 46
parakeet, 27, 58

Parakeet, 58, 70
parental care, 20
Parental care, 14
parrot, 56, 58, 70, 71, 72
parrots, 23
Partridge, 48
Paul Gallico, 55
Paul Sterry, 92
Peacock, 44
pecking, 23
Peeps, 25
Pelican, 38
pelicans, 7, 22
penguin, 60
penguins, 6, 7, 21, 34, 61, 63
Penguins, 34, 48, 60, 63
Peregrine Falcon, 32, 88
Peruvian Pygmy Owl, 47
Pets, 70
pheasant, 58
Pheasant, 8, 39, 45
pheromones, 23
Philippine Eagle, 9
Philippines, 9
Phoebes, 17
phoenix, 67
Phoenix, 67, 68
Pieter Bruegel the Elder, 58
Pigeons, 40
Pine Siskins, 16
Pionus Parrot, 72
Piping Plovers, 16
plumage, 18, 23, 34, 35, 36, 44, 45, 52, 70, 91
plunge-dive, 22
poaching, 9, 10
pollution, 87, 90
preen, 18
Prince, 50

probe, 22
Pygmy Nuthatch, 29, 36
Pygmy Nuthatches, 40
Quail, 8
Quaker Parrot, 71
Quetzal, 39, 44
Rabindranath Tagore, 54
Rails, 35
Rainbow Lorikeet, 45
rainforests, 1, 4, 5
raptors, 6, 84, 86
Rattles, 25
Raven, 27, 53
ravens, 64, 67, 68
Ravens, 17, 64, 67
Red-billed Quelea, 11
Red-breasted Merganser, 32
Red-breasted Nuthatch, 36
Red-naped Sapsucker, 46
Red-winged Blackbirds, 15
rehabilitator, 74
Rhea, 43
Richard Bach, 55
Richard Crossley, 92
Robert Louis Stevenson, 56
robin, 51
Robyn, 49
Roc, 68
Rock Dove, 32
Rock Pigeon, 11
Rock Sparrows, 17
Roger Tory Peterson, 93
Roseate Spoonbill, 38
Rosella, 70
Ruby-crowned Kinglet, 37
Ruby-throated Hummingbird, 15, 29, 42

Rufous Hornero, 17
Rufous-tailed Hummingbird, 15
Rufous-vented Chachalacas, 17
Russia, 10, 66, 67
Sage Grouse, 23
Sahara, 6
Saharan Africa, 11
Salvador Dali, 57
Samurai Jack, 65
Sandpiper, 42
Sandpipers, 35, 41, 49
savannas, 4
Scarlet Macaw, 44
Scavenging, 22
Scott Whittle, 93
Screeches, 25
Seabirds, 7
Seagull, 52, 55
seeds, 20, 21, 36, 37, 40, 89
Senegal Parrot, 72
Shoebill, 37, 39, 44
Siberian Crane, 10, 30
Siberian Tit, 37
Simurgh, 68
Sirens, 69
skeletons, 2
skylark, 54
sleeping, 14
Snow Bunting, 15
Song Sparrow, 42
Song Sparrows, 17
songbirds, 6, 15, 25, 40, 84
songs, 14, 18, 23, 24, 25, 26, 50, 65, 82, 91
Sooty Shearwater, 15
South Africa, 10
South America, 46, 47, 70, 71, 72

Southern Cassowary, 30, 31, 39, 43
Southern Rockhopper Penguin, 43
sparrows, 5, 6, 51
Sparrows, 21, 40, 51
Spoon-billed Sandpiper, 9
Spotted Pardalote, 29
Steve Madge, 93
Steve Miller Band, 50
Sugarbirds, 22
Sumatran Trogon, 47
summer, 52
Sun Conure, 70
sunbirds, 1
Sunbirds, 21
Superciliaried Hemispingus, 46
Swallows, 18, 21
swamps, 4
swan, 52, 66, 67
Swan, 52, 60, 66
swans, 7, 25, 54
Swift, 32
Sword-billed Hummingbird, 37
T.S. Eliot, 53
Tanya Tucker, 51
Tawny-flanked Prinia, 29
Taylor Swift, 49
teach, 20
Ted Hughes, 54
terns, 7
territory, 14, 18, 23, 24, 25, 26
The Beatles, 50
The Lady and the Unicorn tapestries, 58
The Natural History and Antiquities of Selborne, 79

The Trashmen, 50
Theodore Roosevelt, 76
They Might Be Giants, 51
Thunderbird, 68
Tim Birkhead, 92
Tim Burton, 61
Tim Flach, 92
Tinamous, 35, 41
Toco Toucan, 37
Tom McGrath, 63
Tom Ruegger, 62, 63
Tom Stephenson, 93
tools, 14, 78, 80
Tree Swallow, 15
Tree Swallows, 16
Treecreeper, 37
Treecreepers, 40
Trills, 25
Tropicbird, 39
Trumpeter Swan, 30, 31
Trumpets, 25
Tundra Swan, 31, 33
Turacos, 36
Turkey, 7
Turul, 69
Tweety, 61, 62
Twitty, 49
Upcher's Warbler, 46
Urban, 5, 84
urban areas, 5
Victoria Crowned Pigeon, 39
visual displays, 23
Vocalizations, 14, 23
Vulture, 64
vultures, 14, 21
Vultures, 22, 64
W.B. Yeats, 54
wade, 22
Wallace Stevens, 54

Walter Lantz, 62
Warblers, 21
Warbles, 25
warn, 26
Waterbirds, 6
waterfowl, 5, 24, 25, 83, 86
Wendell Berry, 55
Wetlands, 4, 83
Whistles, 25
White-tailed Ptarmigan, 15
White-throated Needletail, 32
White-throated Sparrow, 11, 15, 42
White-winged Triller, 47
Whooper Swan, 31
Whooping Crane, 30, 33
Wildlife Refuges, 83
William Holman Hunt, 58
William Shakespeare, 53
Willow Warbler, 29, 37, 42
Wilson's Warblers, 16
wings, 1, 2, 3, 14, 30, 44, 45, 50, 68, 69
Wings, 2, 3, 48, 73
Wonder Woman, 65
Woodlands, 84
woodpecker, 62
woodpeckers, 16, 22, 24, 25, 36, 84
Wrens, 41
Yardbirds, 49
Yellow Warbler, 42
Yellow-billed Hornbill, 38
Yellow-browed Warbler, 37
Yellow-fronted Canary, 27
Ziz, 69

ABOUT THE AUTHOR

Karen Lee is an avid backyard birder and information enthusiast. To her, birds are not just creatures but a source of joy and wonder.

ALSO AVAILABLE

BIRD SEARCH USA - A Word Search Book for Bird Lovers
Birds are everywhere. Even when you can't see them, you can hear them. The United States enjoys a wide variety of wild birds. This book offers two large print word searches for each US state. These are the birds you would actually find in the state, with the official state bird indicated as well.

WORD NERD USA - United States of America - Themed Word Search Puzzles
This word search book contains puzzles for each state and US territory. There are also broader puzzles for American originated subjects such as food, television, movies, and animals. The large print book also features "mega puzzles" to extend the fun.

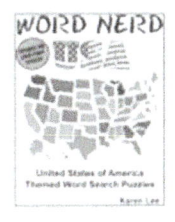

PUZZLED BY THE 80s
The 1980s were a time of massive economic and geopolitical changes. Yeah, we're not going to delve into any of that serious stuff. Instead, this book contains word searches, crosswords, cryptograms, and anagrams all themed around the pop culture of the 80s - movies, music, TV, fads, and more.

PUZZLED BY THE 70s
This book takes all the major pop culture milestones - all the cinematic trends, all the musical stylings, all the popular fads - and tosses them into a blender. Inside, you'll find dozens of word search puzzles, crossword puzzles, cryptograms, anagrams, kriss-kross puzzles, and even a few period-correct logic puzzles.

MOVIE QUOTE CRYPTOGRAMS
This book contains over 500 quotes from movies, ranging from the earliest of talkies to the most recent blockbusters. Some of the quotes are iconic and timeless, while others delve deeper into the movie - it won't be as easy as seeing the title and immediately guessing the quote!

ACADEMY AWARD WORD SEARCH PUZZLES
This book features 100 full size word search puzzles containing nominees for Best Picture, Best Director, Best Actor / Actress and Best Supporting Actor / Actress. The puzzles are broken down on a year-to-year basis so you can see who was up against whom and who took home the trophy. There are also puzzles based on most nominated writers, composers, and more!

Made in the USA
Las Vegas, NV
02 November 2023